# SURVIVING
# The HOLOCAUST:
# The Legacy of Peter Jablonski

D1552728

## John R. McIntyre
## with
## George J. Mandelbaum

Copyright © 2019
ISBN 9781673270471
Library of Congress: TX 8-852-985

Cover Design by John J. McIntyre based on an original  Drawing
from the Recollections of Peter Jablonsky - 1943

# Acknowledgements

The authors wish to express our thanks to several people who have assisted us in preparing this memoir of the experiences of Peter Jablonski, George Mandelbaum, and Walter Saltzberg. We begin by paying special tribute to the foresight and attention to detail exercised by Peter Jablonski a.k.a. Nachman Fryszberg. Given the many innovative ideas and activities that he executed on behalf of relatives, friends and persons unknown, one comes to expect that kind of thorough record from Peter. In fact, he left us 18 single-spaced pages of notes on the experiences of their lives following the German's invasion of Poland. He also provided several on site renderings of the Trawniki Camp and the Hiding Place. Without those notes, written in English for just this purpose, this book would not have been possible.

The members of the Saltzberg family, especially George S. Saltzberg Provided invaluable information about Peter's relationship with his father, Walter Saltzberg. Basia Wojtas was able to fill in vital information regarding Sabina's life and her interaction with Peter during their 60 + years of marriage. We also wish to offer our thanks to Joan Giurdanella for the initial edits for the work. Thanks to her many suggestions and well-researched historical recommendations, the manuscript has been improved from its original version. Credit for the legal counsel associated with this undertaking must be given to Brian Fleisig, Esq., who guided us through the process of creating a limited liability corporation for the book. The company is known as "Peter's Legacy".

We wish to also thank John J. McIntyre, son of John R. McIntyre for designing and formatting the art work for the book's cover and spine. Both of us appreciate the fine work that he provided for us. Finally, we would like to express our gratitude to our wives Patricia and Bonnie for their forbearance when our many meetings replaced time we might have spent with them. Their support and understanding was essential to the task.

## DEDICATION

*To the memory of my dear parents, my family members, and the millions of people killed during the war; to my cousins Edna and Murray Flug in the United States. They were my inspiration to try to survive the war. To my dear wife, Sabina, who stood by my side and supported me as I returned to good health. She contributed to my efforts to overcome obstacles and attain a better life together. To George Mandelbaum and Walter Saltzberg, who are living witnesses to the horrors of the past. To the non-Jews, who were helpful to many others, while risking their own lives.*

*—Nachman Fryszberg, aka Peter Jablonski*

*Peter was an unselfish, caring, and intelligent man with the ability to solve problems that would have unsettled the average person. His circumstances often required immediate action at the risk of his life and the well-being of his companions. Peter was also extremely resourceful. He used the materials that were available to him to create the means of survival. What he did not find, he innovated realizing that his ingenuity could mean the difference between life and death for those in his care. No one appointed or elected him to this duty of caring for others. It was simply what he saw as necessary, and accepted the responsibility to resolve. Peter provided the nucleus of the account that we have recorded in this book. He wanted to make certain that these horrific deeds would always remain evident to the world so that the stain of their occurrences will ensure that they never happen again. We trust that we have provided some measure of assurance that his goal shall become reality.*

*—John R. McIntyre and George Mandelbaum*

# Contents

# Preface

This volume recounts the experiences of one Jewish family, and how some of their members survived, or succumbed, to the evils of the Holocaust. Their survival was, in large measure, due to the ingenuity and persistence of Nachman Fryszberg, aka Peter Jablonski. Nachman assumed the name, Peter Jablonski, when he removed papers from the body of a deceased Polish national. * Those documents enabled him to secure safe passage and to provide for the well-being of several other family and friends in their struggles for survival.

As he recorded his odyssey through occupied Poland in the days before and after his postwar life following escape from the Trawniki labor camp. Peter reflected on his own trials: *"I am purposely not expressing my thoughts and emotions while writing about these experiences. It would be too much for me to bear and I lack the words to describe them. I prefer to restrict myself to the facts. Many of these facts, in their complete detail, remain inexplicable to me. So, I limited myself to summarizing the significant events."* **

What Peter refers to as "inexplicable" is actually the recollections of his emotionally charged experiences. Ultimately, he realized that it was not possible to separate his experiences from his emotions. For example, he recollected, *"I found a leather wallet where I kept my Kennkarte (identification papers). This gave me a push to realize, I am somebody, and that realization helped me to carry on."* The consistent degradation of the Jews by their Nazi tormentors caused many to question their own self-worth. Peter knew the importance of retaining his sense of identity, and he struggled to remain his own person. It is not difficult to imagine the loss of regard for one's self, when one spends his/her more impressionable years being hunted down. The Nazi ideology boosted the advocates' sense of importance by treating non-Aryans as less than human. Peter was able to suppress his emotions because of the need to remain one step ahead of his oppressors for his own survival. All the while, he was trying desperately to protect his companions and family members from cruel and unimaginable dangers.

As he observed his relatives and friends falling victim to their oppressors, Peter remained resourceful and tried to detach himself from the natural emotional reactions associated with his plight. Instead of succumbing to his fears, he tried to focus on survival and protection. This was not always possible. Especially at night when his emotions plagued his efforts to reach a relaxed state. He was often sleep-deprived due to the nature of the tasks he accepted and the vigilance they required. Many nights, he was unable to sleep at all due to the sounds of bombardment and gunfire, or the screams of innocent victims.

Guided by Peter's generous counsel and leadership, family and supporters assumed various vital yet unfamiliar roles, usually at his direction. Peter advised them of the means to overcome the constant threat to their lives. The Nazis assigned Peter and his family to labor concentration camps where they served in the roles of various tradespeople in order to survive. Peter was the constant, the most resourceful, and the last to despair over his circumstances, no matter how dire they seemed. He chose to take on responsibilities he realized were necessary for his survival and that of his fellow fugitives. He knew what techniques to use to hide from the enemy, and he possessed the skills and courage to execute them. Peter was willing to take calculated risks when he understood that their success was vital for the cohort he was protecting. These traits were invaluable for the survival of his fellow victims, in general, and for his family's situation. The following personal credo embodied his attitude regarding the communication of their experiences to the generations that follow: *"Some parents try to hide the truth. Children need to know the truth. If they hide it, another Hitler will come along and say 'it's not true, they only killed ninety-nine people, instead of nine hundred ninety-nine thousand people.' The truth must be revealed. Like religion, if it is written and provided to others, it is more reliable."*

Peter believed strongly that the story of the Nazi atrocities deserved the widest possible circulation. He was committed to telling the truth in all its explicit details to as many people as he could, so that in the telling he would reveal the full extent of the Nazis' evil intentions. He painstakingly recorded his recollection of the horrors he experienced. He did so in order that we might realize and pass along the specifics of those events to ensure that they will never happen again. This publication aims to extend and support Peter's purpose.

As the atrocities became more of a distant reality, many thoughts came to Peter's mind and many questions persisted in search of answers. When he was able to reflect on the events that shaped his life in a less stressful environment, Peter took advantage of the opportunity to evaluate his past and the prospects for the future. By doing so, he gradually attained a modicum of peace of mind through a commitment to passing on an explanation of the events that influenced his life and shaped his values.

*According to his preference and his family's habit, we will refer to Nachman as Peter Jablonski throughout the rest of this narrative.

**Italicized quotations are derived from Peter's notes, unless otherwise indicated.

INTRODUCTION

Getting older, many thoughts and reflections are coming to my mind, not having answers to many

facts, happenings. Perhaps sitting down in a relaxed position, I will clarify to myself, first some

other explanations... and hopefully peace of mind. I am sure, my upbringing at home as a youngster

had a great influence of decision making in and during unusual drastic dangerous situations, I will

introduce a short explanation.

I was born in Lublin, Poland. Attended school, completed high school, and additional
further an n accounting night school. We had a manufacturing of paper goods, for offices and
schools. I had been employed, as well my only sister, and mother too, to maintain a standard. . We
were not deeply religious, but the influence was rooted deeply as to charity, helping, especially in
between family members, whom we had a large number. From my fathers side- sister Mindla
(Greenberg, and his sister Miriam Kacenelenbogen. Mr. Isriel Kacenelenbogen was a known person
with great social activities, before and during the wartime. From my mother's side, most the relative
were in Warsaw, Zamosc. Grabowiec. and other localities Fathers family was in Kowel, but I was
newer there. I do remember, the so many stories father was telling us of the Russians influence and
pogroms, yet He had a self educated higher standard in chemistry and mathematics. Many practical
approaches to solving any difficulties, I learned-adopted from my father.
We had albums of so many family pictures. , I see them only in my mind. . NOW! Frysebergs were a
great family and they corresponded with us. There was also the family Flancman. My father is from
the Fryobergs Mothers family, The Mandelbaums in Warsaw were the center, once was the
Grandmother and the greater number of family members. Elchanon the oldest brother and the head
of the family business, after grandfather passed away. Second brother Chaic, sister Rachel, Esther a
Mindla (from Krakow) was there only ones before the war, but I was there during the war and after
too. Rachel emigrated to U.S.A. before the war we lost our correspondence with the family, only
occasionally we had some news from Warsaw, by word of mouth by some people our home in
Lublin, consisted of a larger room, kitchen and a vestibule. On the main floor of this same location
was our paper goods factory, making assorted goods for offices and schools. I was employed right
after school and so was my only sister and mother too. We had to help out to maintain a standard. I
course at that time there was no T.V. or telephone, not even a toilet in the house or a shower. This
was the so-called "middle class life". Before this manufacturing father had a production of different
shoe paste.
I completed high school and an additional night school of bookkeeping, to help out in our factory.
Father was overworked, I do not remember Him to have any vacation, except the" official holidays

Later on, the A K stopped Her saying "You are a Jewish "KURWA" SHUT AT her killing the dog! Since than She was hiding
in the country side until She died of cancer. We helped Her and the Husband, too.
Many many years later my Sabina was visiting Her parents in Poland, stopped firstly at Mr Pencylinsz, with gifts,
staying there for 2 days,.. and than to the parents.

After all I believe THERE ARE SOME GOOD PEOPLE IN MAJORITY, we may have hope THE HUMAN BEING

WILL LEARN A LOT MORE AFTER MORE THAN FIFTY YEARS. I COULDN'T LEARN
HOW TO STOP LIVING THROUGH IT. !! SO OFTEN AT NIGHTS!!!

PETER JABLONSKI
THORNHILL- ON.
FEB. 18- 2000

*First and last pages of Peter Jablonski's Written Recollections*

Fortunately, for those of us who remain, he left eighteen single-spaced pages of his recollections to provide an anecdotal record of his many encounters during his life. These pages along with recorded interviews, written accounts of the events, and the recollections of Peter's cousin, George Mandelbaum, serve as the main source materials for this memoir. George is now eighty-one years of age. Peter made a promise to George's father, Elchanon Mandelbaum, that he would ensure George's escape from the Warsaw Ghetto and eventual flight to freedom. Peter's childhood upbringing and his propensity for independent thinking filtered his decision-making skills. He found it instructive to recall how those life-threatening situations occupied and influenced his thinking. He often mused about his survival in Poland under the Nazi regime. Peter felt it was very important to pass on a complete and accurate witness to future generations. He did so in order to steel his successors against a repeat of the disrespect for life that marked the German effort to exterminate the Jewish people. He realized that the Nazi ideology encouraged the complete annihilation of the Jews as a "final solution" toward the fulfillment of their doctrine regarding the superiority of the Aryan race.

This book traces events following the Nazi invasion of Poland. Subsequent to the successful takeover of the country, the Nazis began to isolate and liquidate the Jews in part through the establishment of a series of ghettos. We describe the physical and emotional characteristics of the ghetto as well as the punitive encounters between Jews and their Nazi captors. The Mandelbaums became the central family group of this narrative. Specifically, we describe their experiences with murder, slave labor, escape of their youngest member, George Mandelbaum, and the rescue of Walter Saltzberg. These circumstances called upon their instincts for survival and protection as modeled by their orphaned cousin, Nachman Fryszberg, aka Peter Jablonski.

We trace Peter's travels in his effort to avoid capture by the Nazis or their sympathizers and the many hardships that accompanied his odyssey. Finally,

Peter, his documented pseudonym, met the love of his life, Sabina Myszkowska. They married, retrieved his cousin George, and for the second time, Peter arranged for George's safe passage. This time, George traveled to England and subsequently to the United States to live with his other relatives. Peter and Sabina traveled to Israel and ultimately took up residence in Canada. Walter Saltzberg also made his home in Canada, after undergoing several surgeries to assist with his recovery from severe injuries that he suffered during the bombardment of Warsaw. All three principals in the story lost their parents and siblings resulting from the actions of the Nazi oppressors.

This is the tale of one extended family and their members, but it represents the experiences of many Jews at the hands of the Nazi military and civil authorities during World War II. It is our sincere wish that readers of this volume will apprehend the evils of the intent and actions of the Nazi regime and guard against any, and all, similar political ideologies in the future.                    John R. McIntyre and

George J. Mandelbaum - 2019

## Prologue

*"We must not be silent when we see injustices. We must take care of those who need help, and we must not be ashamed to talk about it."*

*—Clemantine Wamariya, Rwandan genocide*

*survivor*

## Antisemitism in Europe

Throughout western Europe and as far east as Russia, the Jewish experience reflected varying instances of antisemitic encounters. By the 1300s, the Jews were a thriving presence in the medieval kingdom that was Poland. In the 1400s, Jews in Spain were required to convert to Christianity, leave the country, or face execution. In Russia and other eastern European countries *pogroms* (physical attacks on Jews) went unchecked by their governments. Jews who lived in small villages called *shtetls* felt the wrath of Russian antisemitic fury. In 1569 a Polish-Lithuanian territory was created to increase political and economic influence for Polish Jewry. In the 16th century, 80% of all the world's Jews lived in Poland. There were over 3 million Jews and 1.9 million non-Jewish Poles inhabiting the country. It was claimed, with demonstrable basis, that Polish culture was in part Jewish culture. However, Jewish successes only caused envy among their countrymen. These animosities were further fueled by the antisemitic stance of the church that dominated Poland at that time.

Anti-Semitism plagued Polish Jewry again as a by-product of the 1648 rebellion in Poland. In the years 1648-49, Jews became victims when the proletariat and the Cossacks revolted against Polish nobility. During that period, the economic decline of the Polish-Lithuanian Commonwealth accompanied a reduction of tolerance for Jews by the Commonwealth's leadership. By the seventeenth century, the Jewish population in Poland had risen to over 300,000. Approximately 100 years later in 1772, the armies of Sweden, the Ukraine, and Russia overran Poland and partitioned the country among the invading nations. As a result, Twenty-five percent of the Polish population was eradicated. The partitioning agreement marked an end to the sovereign nations of Poland and Lithuania for the next 123 years. Simultaneously, the growth of nationalism throughout Europe gave rise to the scapegoating of Jewish inhabitants. Jews were technically "emancipated" in various European countries starting with France in September 1791. Emancipation involved removal of legal discrimination and the granting of full citizenship for Jews willing to swear a loyalty oath to their country of residence. Sadly, formal emancipation did very little to diminish antisemitic activities in those countries.

A set of writings known as "The Protocols of Elders of Zion" claiming a worldwide Jewish conspiracy appeared in France during the 1890s. The protocols were distributed widely, including in America. The 24 chapters, or protocols, claimed a Jewish conspiracy to take over the world, distorting Jewish activity to claim nefarious intentions. The Times of London reported the protocols were plagiarized in their edition of August 17, 1921. However, the writings became one of the foundations of Nazi ideology and the initial suggestion of a "Jewish problem". Hitler quoted the content of the protocols in several speeches. Despite debunking by several nations including Russia and the United States, the protocols were published in several languages and recently have been appearing more frequently on the Internet, sponsored by various antisemitic hate groups.

The Nazis concocted what became known as the "Final Solution" to the "Jewish Problem". When their small-scale firing squads and gas vans became inefficient and psychologically burdensome for the killers, the Nazis opened six major concentration camps (Chelmo, Belzec, Sobibor, Treblinka, Auschwitz-Birkenau, and Majdanek). Approximately three million Jews were gassed in those six camps. By the combination of gassing, shootings, cremation, disease, and starvation a total of over six million Jews were victims of the Nazi regime. That number represented two-thirds of European Jewry.

What had been the heart and soul of Ashkenazi Jewry became a token reminder of their influence. A combination of relocation to the death camps, successful escape, and an inability to account for people's whereabouts all contributed to the decline in the Jewish population. Warsaw was not the sole Polish ghetto. Krakow, Kielce, Czestochowa, Radom, Lodz, and Lublin among others existed as ghettos in Poland, between October 1939 and April 1941. However, Warsaw was the site of the largest number of ghettoized Jews. Currently, only a few thousand Jews from a high point of more than 3.5 million remain in Warsaw. At Warsaw's high point of population only New York City boasted a higher concentration of Jewish people in a single city.

What factors lead to the discriminatory behavior directed toward the Jewish people? For one reason, the Jews were a minority culture within various majority societies. They adhered to a unique set of religious and social practices and, they spoke and wrote in the Yiddish language which further set them apart from the majority. They were also successfully engaged in many respected and enviable occupations and professions. Thus, their success became a source of ill-will among their neighbors. In Europe the dominant religion was Christianity, a fact that isolated the Jews from the prevailing society. Christian churches taught followers that Jews should be blamed for the crucifixion of Jesus Christ. The church's teachings were considered infallible and unquestionable. Jews also fulfilled the role of money lenders; an occupation associated by the Christian Church with the sin of usury. Borrowing and lending, then and now, are vital economic functions that can nevertheless engender resentment toward the lenders. These factors and the political climate that followed the First World War served to make the Jews likely scapegoats. Truthfully, 600,000 Jews saw military service during the First World War. They fought in the Austrian, German, and Russian armies, often fighting against each other. However, the Jews were blamed by the Nazis for Germany's loss in the First World War.

**Polish Jewry**

At the conclusion of World War I, Poland's independence was fully restored. The combination of the World War, the Russian Revolution, and the Treaty of Versailles served to distract the occupying nations and discourage them from interfering with the Polish government. As the Jews were expelled from other European countries, they found acceptance in Poland once more. The Polish-Lithuanian Commonwealth evolved from two separate kingdoms to one state with an elected king. Poland became a hybrid political entity, a democratic monarchy. The most diverse population in Europe resided in Poland. Catholics, Protestants, Muslims, and Jews coexisted in the new political organization. Yet the Jews alone were the only group banned from voting.

The practice of anti-Semitism existed then and continues to this day. It reached its zenith during the rise of the Third Reich as Adolf Hitler brazenly determined that he would orchestrate the extermination of the entire Jewish population. Hitler remained in power from 1933 to 1945. His regime was responsible for the extermination of more than 6 million Jews.

According to the census of 1931, 80 percent of the 3.1 million Polish Jews claimed Yiddish as their native language (Web, 1999). To them, Poland was Polyn, Warsaw was Varshe, and Krakow was Kroke. In 1933 Jews had a presence in every European country. Nine million lived in countries that would be occupied by the Nazis during World War II. Two of every three of these Jews would be killed by the Nazis. In 1939, when there were 3.5 million Jews in Poland, Europe's largest Jewish population, 380,567 of them, more than 30 percent, lived in the capital city of Warsaw.

The Nuremberg laws were approved on September 15, 1935. These initiatives were designed to firmly establish the inferiority of Jews in the eyes of the Third Reich. The Laws defined a Jew as a person with three or four Jewish grandparents. Thus, any individual whose forebears were Jewish became vulnerable to be treated as a Jew by virtue of birth, including some Catholic priests or nuns. These acts added thousands of additional persons to the class of people considered as Jews. The Nazis also insisted on the classification of Jews as a race and not a religion or social group. Thus, their vulnerability was severely increased. In effect, the Third Reich demanded the mandatory retirement of non-Aryan peoples; the suspension of employment of Jewish professionals and academics; and, Citizenship acquired after the outbreak of World War I, August, 1914, was repealed for Jews.

The German war machine invaded Poland on September 1, 1939 and met little resistance from an inept, outmanned, and poorly trained Polish army. It took a mere four weeks for Germany to bring the Polish army to its knees and occupy the capital. Even before the German invasion and subsequent antisemitic rulings the Jews in Poland were experiencing various forms of discrimination. Pogroms were common and, in a single instance between 1935 and 1937, 80 Jews were killed and over 200 injured. Regulations were approved that segregated Jewish university students from their non-Jewish peers. In many cases Jewish students were forced to sit apart from their classmates on separate benches. Finally, boycotts of Jewish businesses were initiated and Poles were encouraged to do business only with non-Jewish merchants. These pre-existing antisemitic circumstances made Poland highly vulnerable to the more extreme, malicious treatment of the Third Reich. Thus, the treatment of the Jews by representatives of many countries and cultures was not unfamiliar to the Mandelbaums or the Fryszbergs. Both families were aware of the signs and the sentiments that comprised antisemitism. However, neither family was prepared for the brutality perpetrated by the Nazi regime.

In spring 1940, the Germans decided to delineate an area of Warsaw to be inhabited predominantly by Jews by building a wall encircling it. They expelled ethnic Poles from their neighborhoods and ordered the relocation of Jews from their existing residences into the city center. The ghetto in Warsaw initially housed 450,000 Jews, who were forced to reside in a limited space and in unreasonably close proximity to one another. The number gradually grew to include Jews transported from other areas of German incursion. The gradual deprivation, starvation, and dehumanizing of the Jewish people crowded into these limited geographical areas made their lives intolerable. The population density of the ghetto was approximately 150,000 persons per square kilometer, or an average of 7.2 people living in each individual room.

In the various ghettos, the Germans established a Jewish council of elders, called the Judenrat, to maintain order, provide services, control sanitation, and affect quarantines. However, these elders were easily manipulated to do the Nazi bidding, no matter how heinous the task. Scorned by the Jews, whom they purportedly protected, this group became the enforcers who arranged for the transportation of people to the trains that took them to "resettlement" camps. One of the leaders of the Warsaw Judenrat was Adam Czerniakow who, after hearing rumors of the deportation of Jews, confronted several members of the German high command. He was told that the rumors were false on July 20, 1942. On July 22, Czerniakow was ordered to assemble 6,000 Jews to the *Umschlagplatz* (an area adjacent to the train station) for deportation by 4:00 p.m. that day, and similar numbers each day thereafter. Understanding that he was expected to be indirectly involved in the murder of Jews, he committed suicide on July 23, 1942. The Judenrat eventually developed a contemptuous reputation even among the Germans by whom it was organized. In fact, the Germans shipped members of the Judenrat out for "relocation" (i.e., liquidation) along with their other victims, when they outlived their usefulness.

Soon after they overran Poland in 1939, the Nazis separated thousands of Jews from their family members and their homes and forced them to reside in the limited conditions of the ghettos. Warsaw was the largest of at least 1,000 ghettos in Poland to experience this imposed set of humiliating living conditions. The Mandelbaum family was shunted from their rather comfortable living quarters at Smulilowskiego Street to the much more crowded location at Nalewki Street. George's father was forced into slave labor at a clothing factory doing jobs for which he lacked experience. George was not allowed to attend school and his play activities became highly restricted for a boy of five years.

## Life in the Ghetto

Young children were especially susceptible to the violent whims of the Nazi soldiers. The Nazis had no respect for young children since, for their purposes, young children were not "productive" members of the ghetto society. In the effort to keep them secure, Jewish parents held their young children close to their sides, making life quite restrictive for their offspring. When the Mandelbaum family was relocated to the Warsaw Ghetto, young George was restricted from leaving home without adult accompaniment.

On one occasion, a young Jewish boy, who was obviously Chassidic, hurried through the streets of Warsaw trying to avoid eye contact with the German soldiers stationed along his route. Unfortunately, he was not, totally, successful. An observant soldier motioned for him to come near. He patted the young man on the head. removed a pair of scissors from his uniform pocket, and proceeded to cut the boy's side locks. As he did so, he laughed at the boy's tears and mocked him for being a *Säugling* (infant) and not a man. Older men had their beards hacked off with bayonets while women had their children ripped from their arms and thrown mercilessly against nearby walls. This was the kind of harassment or murder to which Jews of various ages were often subjected.

Within the confines of the ghetto, life was precarious in many ways. There was the unpredictable cruelty of the German troops, especially the constant threat of the dreaded SS forces. Housing space was extremely restricted. Exposure to the elements, lack of food and water, and illness and death comprised the debilitating conditions in the ghettos. The Jews were required to wear the identifying yellow star with the word *Jude* (German for Jew) to distinguish them and thereby expose them to a variety of cruel treatments. The stars were made of cotton and were intended to demonstrate that Jews were different and inferior. They were publicly humiliated, mocked, beaten, ridiculed, and berated for their appearance and their beliefs. They were unfairly charged with all kinds of antisocial behaviors and treated as less than human. Jews discovered trying to smuggle food or clothing into

Bundesarchiv, Bild 101I-134-0771A-39
Foto: Zermin | Mai 1941

*Courtesy of Bundes Archives; Zeimin, May, 1941*

the ghetto or within its borders were shot on sight. These deplorable conditions resulted in people lying dead or emaciated on the streets within the ghettos.

The Germans punished Jews for simply being non-Aryan, with a unique cultural heritage who practiced a different religion. Many Jews found safety in professing, or actually, converting to Christianity to avoid the restrictions and retribution. The Nazis forced Jews to scrub the dirt from the cobblestone streets in the ghettos with brushes and acid solutions and perform various other servile duties. A British journalist commented about an incident he observed in the Warsaw Ghetto: "Crowds were fighting one another to get closer to the elevating spectacle of an ashen-faced Jewish surgeon on hands and knees. His delicate fingers, which must have made the swift and confident incisions that had saved the lives of many, held a scrubbing brush. A storm trooper was pouring some acid solution over the brush—and his fingers."

Hitler ordered Jews herded into open boxcars and shipped by trains to concentration camps. These detention and labor camps were in reality death camps, where the German SS troops systematically killed millions of Jews in gas chambers or by shooting. They established killing centers in Auschwitz-Birkenau, Belzec, Majdanek, Sobibor, and Treblinka. The complex at Auschwitz was the largest one. The "final solution" for the vast majority of the ghetto inhabitants would be eventual deportation to the death camps, a solution devised by Hitler, and officially ordered by Hermann Goering on July 3, 1941. During 1941, the Jews in Warsaw were required to eke out an existence for themselves in the ghetto. During July 1942, 64,886 Jews were deported from Warsaw. In August 1942, another 130,660 were forced to leave the city. According to the Nazis own statistics between July 22 to September 21, 1942, 253,741 Jews were deported from Warsaw. The vast majority completed their final journey at the death camp of Treblinka. By September, 1942 only 55,000 Jews remained in the Warsaw Ghetto.

The late Peter Jablonski, the older cousin of George Mandelbaum, described the experiences of the Mandelbaum family who, along with many others, were forced to inhabit the Warsaw Ghetto, through his journals and recollections. Peter's actual family name was Nachman Fryszberg. As a result of his ingenuity and concern, young George Mandelbaum, Walter Saltzberg, and others were able to survive the Nazis' cruelty. Alas, most members of their families did not survive. Millions of Jews suffered the fatal and inhumane abuses of the ghettos and concentration camps. Those who did survive struggled, as Peter did, to resolve the question: *"How to stop living through it so often at night?"* Despite his tribulations, Peter retained hope for human kind. He voiced that hope when he said, *"After all, I believe there are a majority of good people among us, [so that] we can maintain hope for all human beings.* " Peter passed away in 2011 at the age of 90. Herein are his reflections on his effort to survive while protecting as many of his family and friends as possible. In particular, this volume recounts the experiences of the Mandelbaum family and Peter's role in the survival experiences and the future of George Mandelbaum and Walter Saltzberg.

*German soldiers parade through Warsaw on October 5, 1939, to celebrate the conquest of Poland*

*(National Archivees and Record Administration)*

# Chapter One

## The Warsaw Ghetto and the Mandelbaum Family

*"Like thousands of ghetto children, cousin Rosa's little boy stopped walking, shriveled, and died."*

*Janina Dawidowicz, Warsaw Ghetto Survivor*

The Germans established the Warsaw Ghetto on Yom Kippur, October 12, 1940. The Nazis deliberately chose the holiest day—the Day of Atonement—to demonstrate their disdain for the Jews. The decree ordered all Jewish residents of Warsaw to move into a designated area of 3.5 square miles sealed off from the rest of the city by a sturdily constructed wall

*Remains of Warsaw Ghetto Wall Courtesy of George Mandelbaum 2001*

11 miles long, 10 feet high, 10.5 inches thick, and topped with glass and barbed wire.

The ghetto itself had two parts, the "small ghetto" on the north side and the "large ghetto" on the south. The Germans built a wooden bridge between the two sides to enable the Jews to cross from one side to the other under the observation of armed guards. Any Jew found crossing the bridge without Nazi approval could be shot on sight. It took seven months to build the wall, and about one year for the Nazis to enforce the boundaries of the ghetto. The construction was largely the product of Polish labor. with the firm of Schmidt and Mustermann supervising the work. The same firm would cooperate with the Nazis in the building of the Treblinka death camp two years later. To add insult to injury, the Polish Jews were assessed 1.3 million zloty to bear the cost of building the wall.

The ghetto effectively restricted 33 percent of the population to 3 percent of the area of Warsaw. Jewish businesses were shuttered, and food became quite scarce. Importing of food supplies into the ghetto was not permitted and the Nazis rationed what did get through in very limited allotments. Hunger soon became a major issue in combination with the constant danger of contagious illnesses due to deplorable living conditions. Peolple roamed the streets collecting discarded food to satisfy their hunger. Children were banned from roaming the streets begging or pilfering food. If they did so, and were caught, they were subject to being shot on sight. Public kitchens were established where people could line up for the possibility of a portion of soup, without the luxury of a piece of bread to go with it.

In Warsaw, the ghetto wall surrounded the area where many Jews already resided. Therefore, many were not uprooted and the ghetto was more livable because it was already the location of many residents.

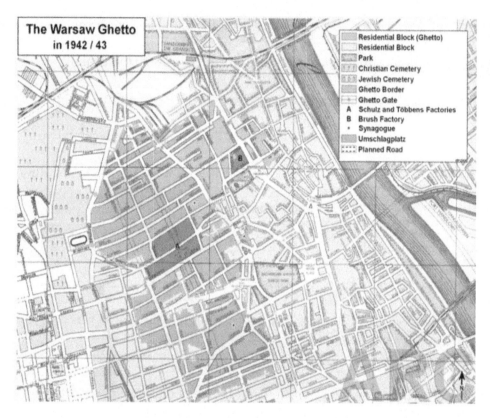

-*Map of the Warsaw Ghetto, 1942–1943. Courtesy of Encyclopedia of Holocaust US Holocaust Museum*

The Germans, however, gradually downgraded the living conditions and means of survival. They forced several families to live in a single apartment. Plumbing was unreliable. Human waste and garbage littered the streets.

Disease was rampant and readily spread due to the cramped, unsanitary living conditions. People were constantly suffering from a lack of sufficient and healthy food. Some, who could, had to pay for food with their limited funds. Others stole or smuggled food into the Ghetto from the Aryan sections. Little fuel for heating was available and clothes were not sufficient to keep bodies warmed. Education was prohibited in the Ghetto although some adults organized classes where possible. Each day yielded more and more orphans with little ability to care for them. This was the way of life in the Ghetto; not only in Warsaw but throughout the ghettos of Europe.

George Mandelbaum was born on December 31, 1937, in Warsaw. He was the only child of Chaia Esther Tyramontov and Elchanon Mandelbaum. Elchanon was born in Zamosc, Poland and Chaia, his mother, was also born and raised in Zamosc. However, they met in Warsaw where they were wed. George reports that it is likely his father attended high school, but he cannot be certain. He lost track of his father at the age of six years. His father's import and export business took Mr. Mandelbaum all over the world. Elchanon dealt in gold, silver, diamonds, watches, religious articles and a varietyof custom designed jewelry. His sister, Rachel recalls that occasionally he placed several watches on her arm so she could provide a display for his customers. He visited the United States several times between 1925 and 1939. In 1939, he made his last visit traveling aboard the

SS *Batory* a Polish ocean liner, from Danzig, Poland to the port of New York.(See: Ship's Manifest below) His business dealt in highly valuable precious metals that earned his family financial security. His partner was a Polish Gentile businessman whose name could not be found.

Elchanon financed Murray Flug, his sister's son in 1934 followed by his sister Rachel and her husband Abraham Flug in 1938, when they moved

*Manifest for SS. Batory listing Elchanon Mandelbaum*

from Poland to the United States. They settled in the Brighton Beach section of Brooklyn, New York. Murray, and his wife, Edna, would eventually become the guardians responsible for the care and development of George Mandelbaum, Elchanon's sole heir. George's father also helped arrange for his two cousins, Sarah and Esther Mandelbaum, to settle in Mexico when the Germans began their military threats prior to the outbreak of war in Poland . Esther had two children, Jaime and Olga Graber. Sarah had three children. They are Jorge, Jaime, and Dorita Renner. All five children were of Mexican birth.

Elchanon traveled quite a bit not only to North America but also in the Middle East. Wisely his father decided to secure a birth certificate written in Cyrillic stating in part that Elchanon was entitled to a Polish passport, making travel more readily available for him. On his last trip to New York in 1939, Elchanon visited his sister Rachel in Brooklyn, New York, and then returned to Poland to gather his family together and leave for the United States to join them. However, the war broke out before he could accomplish the transfer of his immediate family to safety in America.

*Rachel ( Elchanon's Sister) and Elchanon (George's Father) in USA (1939)*

*Letter verifying Elchanon's*
*Visit to USA in 1939*

The family lost contact with Rachel when the war broke out, except for

occasional information they acquired about her American family by mail.

Only Peter retained an awareness of their contact information. Rachel

discontinued her involvement with Elchanon's partner in the sales force

operation of Elchanon's international business when she settled in the

States. Previously, Elchanon traveled wherever necessary to acquire

precious metals and then distributed them to his partner's shop. From there

the goods were delivered to outlets where Rachel would sell to customers.

*George's Father Riding a Camel during a Business Trip to Isrrael*

The Mandelbaum family, who lived in a more upscale area of Warsaw at Smulilowskiego 7, had to leave their attractive middle-class residence and move to the ghetto one night in late 1940 or early 1941. Their former building became administrative offices for the Nazi high echelon. A large swastika was imprinted on the roof of the building to exempt it from the Luftwaffe's bombing raids. Therefore, it was spared and remains to the present day. Elchanon Mandelbaum was a highly successful businessman by Polish standards. In 1930, Elchanon had purchased the four-story building where his family resided for the equivalent of $42,000 and had renovated the building to pristine condition, with twenty-one apartments in the first four floors. He and his family occupied a portion of the second floor. While some items from Elchanon's precious metals business were located in the building, his main inventory was located in the store within his parent's home at Nalewki 41. It was a thriving enterprise until the Nazis confiscated much of his inventory and forced him into slave labor elsewhere. In point of fact, George has been pursuing a legal action against the Polish government for over 50 years in an effort to reclaim the value of the property at Smulilowskiego 7. The Polish government has sold part of the building as condominiums for which they receive financial remuneration. George seeks to recover the value of his father's investment in that facility.

The Mandelbaums had anticipated their displacement from the apartment at Smulikowskiego 7 into the ghetto for a while, so their belongings were partially packed. They grabbed their suitcases or threw them out the windows to the street below. The Nazis herded them like cattle barking directions and demanding that they march to one of the several entranceways into the ghetto. The Mandelbaums joined the rushing crowd, but George's father knew exactly where he intended to take them—to his parent's residence, his former place of business at Nalewki 41. This property was situated in what had now become the Jewish ghetto. (Interestingly, the first Jews murdered in the ghetto were tenants (fifty-three of them) at Nalewki 9). The German soldiers, rifles poised, screamed epithets at George's family and insulted them because of their Jewishness. "*Raus!*

*Raus!* (Out! Out!)", they shouted. George remembers clutching his father's hand and being frightened by the anxiety on his mother's face.

The Mandelbaums recovered most of their possessions and rushed to occupy the building at Nalewki 41, which included a commercial shop in one part of the building. They shared the residence with George's paternal grandmother Matla. Since the Nazis did not care where the Jews took up residence in the ghetto, Elchanon felt they would be most comfortable with his family. George's grandfather had died before the ghetto was established in Warsaw, and Matla's failing health would only be exacerbated by conditions in the ghetto. Eventually, several additional relatives and close friends moved to that location. They included Elchanon's younger brother, Chaim, and his sister, Mindla from Krakow, as well as his nephew and niece Nachman (Peter Jablonski) and Regina Fryszberg from Lublin.

*George's Aunt Rachel with Grandmother Matla Mandelbaum*

Because Elchanon had a successful business, his family enjoyed a rather

comfortable existence before the Nazis' rise to power. When the SS troopers

invaded the Mandelbaum household on that frenetic evening, his

merchandise was seized. But Elchanon had anticipated the confiscation of

the inventory by the Germans, so he forwarded many of his precious metal

holdings from the store located at Nalewki 41 to his Polish gentile partner.

His partner stocked his showroom with them outside the ghetto in the Aryan

sector, where Jews were forbidden to venture. In this manner, their earnings remained solvent and hidden from the ever-covetous Nazi SS troops. Some of those monies would serve as reimbursement for the brave people who enabled his son, George, to escape and travel from Poland to freedom. After Elchanon's death, his Polish partner made most of the financial arrangements for George's safe passage.

In September 1941, the Fritz Schultz Company, a German fur manufacturer, was granted permission to locate their business in the Warsaw Ghetto. The Schultz factory was established in Warsaw in the summer of 1941. By spring 1942, Schultz and his partner, Walter Többens, employed 3,000 slave laborers, all of them were imprisoned Jews who accepted the work because they had no choice. The only way to avoid forcible exclusion from Warsaw, they decided, was to work *for* the Germans. When the ghetto was reduced in size so that two families were confined to a single room, many decided it was time to change their life style in order to survive. In contrast with his previous existence, George's father was forced to become one of the slave laborers. On some days he worked for twenty hours per day at the manufacturing division run by Fritz Emil Schultz at Nowolipie 44 inside the Warsaw Ghetto The factory made clothes shoes, leather products, sweaters, and socks for the German soldiers. This was an ovewhelmring transformation for Elchanon who had been a shrewd entrepreneur and highly successful salesperson not used to heavy physical labor.

The Warsaw Ghetto became a place of extreme poverty. Many of its residents were nearly, or actually, starving. Meals at the Mandelbaum's residence gradually diminished from acceptable portions of meat and vegetables with bread to very little meat, if any, and some bread. Nevertheless, George recalls his mother putting out food portions on the window ledge for those less fortunate than her family. When George ventured outside his mother filled his pockets with treats to share with the less fortunate children. Identifiable non-Aryans could be killed deliberately and violently for little or no rational excuse. Because of the cruelty of the Nazis, especially toward young children, it was not safe for a five-year-old to venture out alone.

George Mandelbaum was a very active and inquisitive child. Due to the circumstances in the ghetto, he was constantly chastised by his mother and grandmother for typical childhood play. Riding his tricycle in the neighborhood became a dangerous and highly restricted activity. George's father would frequently warn him against venturing too far from their Nalewki 41 residence. In fact, he made George promise not to leave the house without him, or his mother. Presciently, he advised George of the unpredictable volatility of the German soldiers. Such regulations became particularly loathsome for a child with George's level of enthusiasm.

One of his most vivid youthful recollections was Grandmother Matla's constant admonishment for what should have been a typical activity for a child his age—riding his tricycle around the inside of the house. It may have been safe and George's only alternative but it was, nonetheless, annoying to her. She was fearful that the slightest extraordinary disturbance might bring down the wrath of the volatile Nazi soldiers on their home.

# Chapter Two

## The Lublin Ghetto and the Fryszberg Family

*"Years can go by, but your memory will not fade. Certain events, if they are extraordinary, you never forget them. They're etched in your brain and they stay with you for the rest of your days."*

*Kitty Hart-Moxon, Lublin Ghetto and Auschwitz Survivor*

Nachman Fryszberg, aka Peter Jablonski, was born in the city of Lublin, Poland, on October 20, 1920. In 1939, the city's population was 122,000 with 42,830, or 30 percent, identifying as Jewish. At that time, Jews owned over 50 percent of the workshops and 30 percent of the factories in the town of Lublin. Lublin is situated approximately 106 miles southeast of Warsaw. Peter's residence in Lublin was a meager one. His family lived in an apartment at 24 Lubartowska Street (See photo) that consisted of a large family room, a kitchen, and a vestibule. There were no modern amenities such as, a telephone, a shower, not even toilet within their living quarters. Peter's father, Yankel Fryszberg, operated a paper goods factory on the ground floor of the building. He prepared and supplied paper products to schools and offices in the area.

*The Fryszberg Residence at Lubartowska 24*
*Courtesy of George Mandelbaum 2001*

Peter graduated from the gymnasium (high school) in Lublin, where he also studied bookkeeping in the evening to enable him to assist with his father's business. Yankel, his father, employed all of the members of the family in his company in order to ensure that the quality of their products maintained a high level. Peter and his sister, Regina, worked alongside their father and mother after school, whenever possible. Their contributions assured Peter's father that the business would remain a continual source of family income and pride. Many years later, Peter, remarked, *"We were not a particularly religious family, but we possessed a deep commitment to the welfare of our family members."* Although their resources were limited, they freely shared them with others. He confided, *"We never ate alone. There was usually at least one other family member or friend at our dinner table."*

Peter's mother's family, the Mandelbaums, lived in several Polish cities at varied times of her life. Ettle was born in Zamosc in southeastern Poland and then the family moved to Warsaw to join her brother, Elchanon, before she married Peter's father, Yankel Fryzsberg, in Grabowiec, a village in Zamosc County, fifteen miles southeast of Lublin. Eventually, they moved to the city of Lublin. Peter realized that, in her heart, his mother valued her attachment to her large family, as evidenced by the letters written in Yiddish to and from her sister Rachel and her brother Elchanon, and his wife, Chaia Esther, in Warsaw.

Yankel's family originated in the city of Kovel in northwestern Ukraine. Among the family members were his father's sisters Mindla Fryszberg Greenberg and Miriam Fryszberg Kacenelenbogen and Miriam's husband, Israel Kacenelenbogen. Israel was a well-known social activist whose political philosophy directly opposed the Nazis. He was renowned for his left-leaning involvement in Poland before and during the war. Theirs was a small but proud family, and Peter's father considered the family business a focal point of involvement for his wife and children.

Yankel recounted stories to his children of the Russian influence in his home city of Kovel, where his family lived. He told of the many pogroms and the Russian dominance that persisted in that area of the Ukraine. Despite a difficult childhood, Yankel achieved a comprehensive understanding of chemistry and mathematics through self-learning. Peter attributed his refined problem-solving skills to the influence of his father's intellect. He regularly corresponded with the Fryszberg side of the family, particularly his great-grandmother. Their numerous family photograph albums etched the memories of his family into his brain, particularly past events which developed a strong sense of nostalgia within him. These traits enabled him to recall his many experiences in the year 2000 as he wrote his notes about the events he encountered during the war. They were a devoted and proud family. The Fryszbergs were also close to their Flancman cousins, until the Flancmans moved to Palestine in 1938 prior to the start of the War and before Israel became an independent state. Marvin Flancman, a distant cousin of Peter who later took up residence in Canada, became a successful attorney. In the future, he would represent Peter's interests in several real estate matters. However, the Mandelbaums of Warsaw were the stable and most successful center of the family. Therefore, their home in the Warsaw Ghetto became the location where several endangered family members took refuge. Peter traveled to Warsaw on two occasions during the war, when he stayed in the Mandelbaum household; and, after the war, when he reunited with young George Mandelbaum in his Warsaw apartment.

The Germans invaded Lublin on September 18, 1939 when Peter was eighteen years of age. Later in 1939, the Nazis established a ghetto in

Lublin and crowded its Jews within the boundaries. Peter's family had lived what he referred to as "the middle-class life." They were not overly comfortable but they were satisfied with their lot in life. Before his father established the paper goods factory, he owned a paste production company for application in the making and repairing of shoes. Yankel Fryzsberg insisted, "We are not poor." However, he was constantly overworked. Peter could not remember his father ever taking a vacation, except as required on the High Holy Days. *"We were not religious, but we tried to keep up the traditions,"* Peter reported.

As the ghetto became more restrictive, the "good life" began to deteriorate rapidly. Food became less and less available. Meat was rationed very sparingly and when it was available, it was in small portions heavily laced with a watery soup. Peter secured his first job, distributing food to poor people in the Lublin Ghetto, through the intervention of his uncle Israel Kacenelenbogen. The job terminated after a short time. Apparently, providing sustenance to the despised Jews was not in keeping with the Germans' intent for the final solution. The Lublin Jews could not be certain of what the next day, or the next minute, would bring. The Germans became more prone to violence toward them. The object of their consistent ire was the mere visibility of the hated non-Aryan inhabitants of Lublin. Beatings and murders were prevalent. Sanitation conditions became intolerable. Sickness was commonplace, often in epidemic proportions.

Before his family could affect the move to another town, the Nazis began the deportation of Jews from the Lublin Ghetto to concentration camps on March 17, 1942. The circumstances in these labor camps with their poor living conditions and lack of proper nutrition were the cause of many diseases. Despite these circumstances, certain key thoroughfares were designated "off-limits" for Jews. In addition, hundreds of patients in the Jewish hospitals on Lubartowska Street were removed and shot and killed in the Niemce Forest, 15 kilometers from Lublin. Lubarkowska was the street where Peter lived. He could hear the reports of the rifles above the protests of devastated parents.

In 1939 there was over 42,000 Jews in Lublin, or 34% of the 122,000 inhabitants. Lublin, a thriving Jewish community and center of culture, was forced to pay 300,000 zloty as a contribution for the German Army. These were the same German troops that threw their complete Talmudic collection out the windows of the Talmudic Academy and set them afire to burn for over 20 hours. At least 100,000 Jews from Lublin were killed in the Sobibor camp, between May 1942 and January 1943. Peter decided that eventually he would have to leave his home city of Lublin, and escape if he wished to survive and avoid being sent to the death camps.

As conditions grew worse and a secure hiding place was necessary, Yankel Fryszberg built an artificial wall for his family with a secret room in their basement where eight to ten people could hide, if necessary. Being out on the street was so uncertain that this covert location became a necessary component of their living space. The arrangement was temporarily effective until they had to consider a more permanent move to avoid discovery as the size of the ghetto diminished systematically. Peter would later apply his father's creative design to build a hiding place with a faux wall for his own survival.

Winter was very cold in the ghetto because the Germans limited fuel for proper heating. Peter recalled having to burn some of their furniture to cook their scarce food and to keep themselves warm. They found it difficult to sleep at night due to the freezing weather and fear of the unpredictable Nazis and the anxiety-filled days ahead of them. Uncertainty ruled the day. The mental anguish related to avoiding the wrath of their German occupiers was excruciating. In some cases, it caused Jews to harbor mistrust indiscriminately. Due to the uncertainty that marked the effort to survive in an environment populated by so many untrustworthy entities (SS officers, German Army troops, Ukrainian mercenaries, the Polish police, and even their fellow Jews who might turn in their own compatriots to survive), insecurity was rampant.

Their unwillingness to depend on anyone else was unprecedented. When self-preservation is a constant concern, one is reluctant to trust anyone who might betray one's effort to survive. George Mandelbaum reported that it took him a long time before he could trust anyone. Like his cousin Peter, he questioned each and every acquaintance's motivation and feared that they might represent a threat to his safety. They were both challenged to assess who could be relied upon for valid information and advice. These considerations could mean the difference between life and death. Living with these fears would cause anyone to mistrust those whose relationship is not totally familiar. As Richard Rashke claims in *Escape from Sobibor*, "Jews had to learn to distrust in order to survive."

*Regina, their Mother, and Peter Prior to the War*
*From the Collection of Peter Jablonski*

# Chapter Three

## Peter's Escape from the Lublin Ghetto

*"Silence is never the answer ... the opposite of love is not hatred, but indifference."* —*Elie Wiesel, Holocaust survivor and Nobel Prize winner*

In spring 1940, the Nazis confiscated the machinery from Yankel Fryzsberg's paper factory at Lubartowska 24. Soon after that, as two families were forced to live in a single room, Peter's family decided they *had* to move. In April 1942 before his parents could arrange the move, the Germans captured them. They were put into a closed truck supposedly designated for shipment from Lublin to a work camp. However, the Nazis had engineered the truck so that its tail pipe turned carbon monoxide exhaust on the Jews crammed inside. The carbon monoxide gas killed them all and the Nazis buried them in a mass grave in the Krempiec Forest. Peter discovered the whereabouts of his parents' grave by researching the incident after the war. The Lublin Ghetto gradually diminished in population, and as the population lessened, opportunities for work to avoid captivity diminished. After his parents' execution by the Nazis in 1942, Peter's decision to leave Lublin with Regina became much more urgent. More and more of Lublin's Jewish residents were "relocated" to the various death camps, or, like his parents, murdered where they lived.

Peter's first job concluded when the Germans no longer chose to distribute food to the needy. They captured Peter later in 1942 and assigned him to a large work camp in Majdanek-Tarski, known as Deutsche Ausrüstungswerke (DAW). DAW was a subcamp of the dreaded Majdanek death camp. It was a camp for tradespeople, and the Nazis assigned Peter to the print shop, since he possessed the skills that he had learned in his father's paper goods business. Later, he was transferred to the woodworking section in the same barracks. It turned out that his direct boss at that location, Mr. Katz, had been a friend of Yankel's from Grabowiec. The mission of this camp was the production of building materials for the use of the German army. Jewish prisoners of war supervised the daily operation of the camp. The POWs wore German army-type uniforms that were devoid of belts for weapons or any particular military markings.

The leader of the POWs was a man named Fischer, and his assistant was Beno Richter. Beno knew Peter and revealed to him that they were cousins. Beno also informed Peter that Yankel had lived near him in Kowel. Beno advised Peter that he would protect him with a warning, when he sensed impending danger. He had a better vantage point to gather useful information since he managed the kitchen and was often permitted to leave the camp to shop for foodstuffs. That responsibility gave Beno access to outside information on a regular basis.

Another POW, Cwi Zylerberg, knew that Peter's family was supportive of Betar, a Zionist group Peter's uncle Israel Kacenelenbogen also supported. He decided to befriend Peter. On one occasion, Cwi arranged for Peter to visit Lublin as a member of a DAW work group that traveled near his

**MAJDANEK ENVIRONS, FALL 1943**

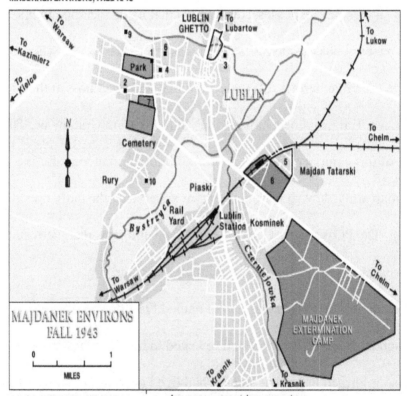

1. Headquarters of Odilo Globocnik (Higher SS and Police Leader of Lublin)
2. Headquarters of the Sipo and SD
3. Zamek Prison(Fortress Prison)
4. Headquarters for Aktion Reinhard
5. Maidan Tatarski Ghetto(Apr.-Nov. 1942)
6. Majdanek Camp Administration(1941-1943)
7. Majdanek Subcamp, 7 Lipowa Street German Armament Works (DAW) P.O.W. Camp for Jews in the Polish Army (December 1939)
8. Majdanek Subcamp (SS Clothing Works and DAW)
9. Majdanek Ogrodkowa Street Subcamp
10. Majdanek Rury Subcamp

US Holocaust Memorial Museum

former home. Zylerberg helped many other Jews, but he was viewed with some skepticism due to his curious relations with the Nazis. He had often been associated with certain Nazi SS officers named Barteczko and Napierala, occasionally riding on motorcycles with them in Lublin as Yankel had mentioned to his son. Peter wondered, *Why is Cwi so often on a motorcycle with the German SS officers?*

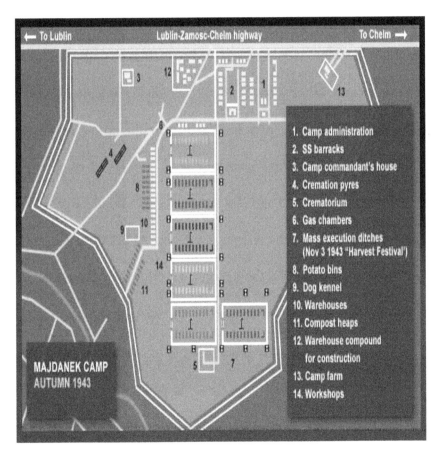

*Majdanek Death Camp, 1943, Courtesy of US Holocaust Museum*

41

Ultimately, remembering his father's skepticism, Peter refused Cwi Zylerberg's offer for safe passage from the DAW. On the other hand, he felt comfortable with the reliability of Beno's advice, and he chose to take his recommendations.

One day, Beno came to Peter with a warning, "There is getting to be a shortage of food." This was a reliable and useful bit of information because Beno was in charge of the kitchen and knew the camp menus. He informed Peter that there would be a forced reduction in food choices. Peter believed him because as the assistant to the Jewish POW leader Fischer, Beno was in a position to order the food and set up the rationing limits. He was attempting to heighten Peter's awareness that a food shortage was the first sign that the camp would soon be abandoned and its inhabitants liquidated, or sent to the death camp at Majdanek. At best, starvation would be the anticipated outcome of a food shortage. Eventually, Beno knew that food would be unavailable for the expendable Jewish prisoners.

Beno determined that Peter did not appear to be sufficiently responsive to his warning. Therefore, early the next morning without advanced notice, Beno forcibly shoved Peter into a large stack of window frames. This unusually harsh diversion, without the benefit of an explanation, was his warning to Peter of the probable liquidation of all prisoners. As Peter hurriedly picked himself up from the rubble of the window frames, Beno advised him, sotto voce, that he had to make an immediate decision.

Beno insisted that it would be to Peter's clear advantage to escape rather than remain in DAW and avoid the risk of transfer to the death camp at Majdanek. Without much time to assess the situation, Peter agreed that he would attempt to escape. He remained at the lower level of the room where they could discuss Beno's plans for his departure. Caution was the watchword of all planning under these circumstances. Peter was constantly challenged to discern who was trustworthy and who could not be trusted. Healthy skepticism characterized all of his plans and actions. In this situation, he considered whether he would be wiser to remain in the camp and take his chances for survival until the camp actually closed, or to risk an uncertain means of escape. He decided not to wait.

Peter decided to follow Beno's plan for escape trusting he could soon reunite with his sister, Regina. In the very early morning with two other prisoners of war and Beno as their guide, the escapees, armed only with garden tools, scurried past the German commandant's building near the main gate of the camp. Beno had prepared a detailed plan that included climbing the wild vines that covered the high brick wall bordering the camp's entrance. As skinny and sickly as he was, Peter managed to convince himself that he could scale the wall. The first POW climbed the wall, but

Peter was unable to make the climb under his own power, so the third POW raised him up from the rear and the first POW pulled him up from the top. Once they reached the other side of the wall, Beno had instructed them to run away from the DAW camp, going in separate directions. Peter assessed the situation and decided to *walk* among the local workers who were on the nearby street. He walked straight ahead, keeping his head erect as if he belonged with the laborers and was heading for his daily job. By following this plan, he was able to escape and avoid his certain demise, transfer to the Majdanek death camp.

Once again, Peter's instincts were correct. Running would have called attention to him as a fugitive. His kind of sixth sense in the face of threat is what kept him alive. He was able to temper his fears with a high level of problem solving and an ability to anticipate his enemy's strategy. He never underestimated the Germans' cunning or let himself accept defeat at their hands. Now, he went about the task of reuniting with his sister, Regina. To accomplish her release, he would have to travel a great distance on foot. These circumstances did not deter Peter from the effort to reunite with his beloved sister. He unrelentingly focused his efforts on finding Regina, above all else. The walk would be strenuous, but his purpose and resolve were indefatigable.

Not knowing what danger he might face, Peter decided to attempt to retrieve Regina and set out with her to join the remaining members of their family 106 miles away in the Warsaw Ghetto. Peter knew that the Nazis placed Regina in a separate camp outside of Lublin, an agricultural camp working with older women. He felt confident that Regina and he would be welcomed by the Mandelbaums, and that Warsaw would be an improvement over Lublin. Thus, Peter began his rather circuitous journey to Warsaw.

# Chapter Four

## The Trek to Warsaw

*"First they came for the socialists, and I did not speak out—because I was not a socialist.*

*Then they came for the trade unionists, and I did not speak out—because I was not a trade unionist.*

*Then they came for the Jews, and I did not speak out—because I was not a Jew.*

*Then they came for me—and there was no one left to speak for me."*

—Martin Niemöller, Lutheran Pastor

After fleeing to relative safety and as he sought to rejoin Regina, Peter reflected on the emotions associated with his recent events, especially the tragedies that affected his family members. He thought about his parents' murder, his experiences at the DAW camp, his escape from DAW, the narrow avoidance of Majdanek's certain death, and his present effort at reuniting with his sister, Regina. In his own words, he expressed these emotions: *"There are within me strong feelings of family unity that I inherited from my mother. Oftentimes, I overheard my mother emotionally reading letters from her sister, written in Yiddish. Near the end of the war, I imagined I could relate everything we went through to members of our family."*

Peter continued on what turned out to be a walk of many miles to locate his sister, Regina. It was on this sojourn that he came across the body of a Polish national with useful identification documents. He was able to retrieve the documents from the body of Piotr (Peter) Jablonski. These identification papers designated him as a non-Jew, so he could use the papers to be eligible for employment in one of the few work opportunities in the ghetto. From that point forward, he began to disguise his identity using the documents that he found to verify his pseudonym.

He knew that Regina was being held in a farming camp for women with a large group of mostly older females well beyond the borders of the city of Lublin. He continued walking at a steady pace in the hope of reuniting with her as soon as possible so they might begin their journey to Warsaw. When he arrived, he found a hiding place in a cluster of bushes near the camp. He secreted himself in the bushes from where he might observe the women passing. He remained there and slept only briefly. As the sun rose, he watched for Regina hoping she would soon pass by. He had a very distinctive whistle that he knew she would recognize. When he spied her, he pursed his lips and whistled softly to attract her attention. She recognized the sound as unmistakably Peter's whistle, and she responded immediately. Regina quickly and quietly let the group get ahead of her and ran to join him among the bushes.

They dared not even risk sharing tears as Peter informed her that their parents were killed and how their murder took place. He held Regina close to him as he explained what he had encountered to get to her. He explained that she, too, would soon find herself threatened and she needed to be on her guard. He also warned Regina of the ruthlessness of the Nazis and their fate should they be caught. He told her that the Germans had designated Lublin to become "free of Jews." He explained that this meant their lives were in danger if they remained there. They arranged to meet at the earliest opportunity and escape to Warsaw.

Regina had no identification that would be acceptable to the Germans; and Peter did not have contact with anyone who might forge such documents to assure their safety. Regardless of the risks they faced, they saw no alternative but to attempt to escape to Warsaw. Without hesitation and lacking authentic identification papers for Regina, they decided to seek shelter with their relatives, the Mandelbaums. Elchanon Mandelbaum, George Mandelbaum's father, was their mother's brother. They felt assured they would be welcomed and safe in their uncle's household. Absent even a temporary place to hide in safety, they proceeded directly to the train station, bought a ticket, and boarded a train to Warsaw. They wrapped their only remaining possessions in a single small package that Peter held firmly in his hands. They had to avoid Nazi storm troopers patrolling the station and at various locations along the train route. These possible encounters provided numerous tense moments. Following a journey of several hours, with great relief, and a good degree of uncertainty, Peter and Regina finally arrived in Warsaw.

Upon their arrival, the two siblings found a bustling city with many automobiles, shopping areas, and people roaming the streets. From their location on the perimeter of the city, they searched for the actual boundaries of the ghetto so they could identify a place to enter without arousing suspicion. This was unfamiliar territory for them, and they sensed the dangers of their surroundings. However, they realized they could not ask directions for some elements of the populace could not be trusted. There were desperate and devious people who might readily reveal the pair's identity for just a kilogram of sugar.

They had ridden all night on a very slow train, and they walked searchingly almost the entire next day. They knew they were getting close to a ghetto entrance when they saw groups of Poles gathering near a brick wall waiting for the emerging workers so they could barter with them for food. They selected a large group to join and followed them through a gate in the wall into the ghetto. Peter knew he had to find Nalewki 41, the Mandelbaum residence. He remembered the address because he had prepared envelopes for his mother who regularly sent letters to her family in Warsaw. As they wandered about the ghetto, they could see the many starving, downtrodden residents searching or begging for food. People were lying in the streets hungry and clinging to the last vestiges of their lives. Peter hustled Regina through the ghetto's streets rather than frighten her by lingering over these sights. Finally, they came upon the Mandelbaum's place of residence.

The Mandelbaums welcomed them. Some family members were familiar; others were not. In the small house, they found Aunt Chaia Esther and Uncle Elchanon, George's mother and father, George Mandelbaum (age five), their grandmother Matla Mandelbaum, the Greenbergs (Mindla, Szyja, and their son), and Esther Mandelbaum, the sister of Elchanon and Peter's late mother. It was a time of great excitement when Peter and Regina arrived at their new home in the heart of the Warsaw Ghetto. They were welcomed graciously and quizzed about their journey. Some relatives asked, "Where are your mother and father?" They avoided responding directly being reluctant to upset their grandmother, who they realized was quite ill. Finding the words to explain the situation that took their parents from them would have been difficult and disturbing to reiterate, especially to a frail grandmother. Therefore, they avoided speaking of their parents' loss, especially in her presence. Peter did confide the circumstances of his parents' murder to his Uncle Elchanon.

It seemed to Peter that life within the Mandelbaum household was proceeding as normal as possible, under the circumstances. The house was clearly overcrowded, and some relatives were known to the two orphaned cousins only by their names. They exchanged information regarding their experiences and heard about those of their extended family. They also expressed their sincere intent to be useful to their relatives during the time of their stay. Peter, at twenty-two years of age, made an almost immediate connection with young George who, at age five, adored his much older cousin almost from the moment he arrived. They began to establish a strong bond that would become a great advantage for George.

Peter engaged George in a variety of activities and became his constant companion and trusted teacher. He encouraged George's propensity for drawing. He taught George basic mathematics and told him stories that enthralled the young boy. Peter enjoyed teaching almost as much as learning. Sometimes he would make up assignments for George to round out his education. George also created his own games to occupy himself. Peter instructed George in the need for absolute silence when it was necessary to avoid confrontation with the Nazis. They practiced these silent drills frequently. Peter warned George of the ruthless and alien nature of the

German soldiers. George learned to trust Peter's judgment. On the other hand, Peter taught George to exercise a healthy mistrust of others while maintaining a high level of anxiety and anger over his circumstances. Trust was constantly at issue and it was viewed as a questionable commodity. George learned to survive by listening and watching carefully before speaking of sentiments when others may overhear him.

Soon after his arrival, Peter tried to convince George's father and the gathered household members of the atrocities that were occurring in the concentration camps. His uncle could not accept such stories of cruelty. In fact, he and his brother Chaim took Peter aside one evening and admonished him to cease telling upsetting tales of the camps for there were some among them who did not believe that the Nazis were capable of mass killings. Elchanon and Chaim did not want to upset their relatives with their nephew's disturbing tales, which some were reluctant to accept. Despite the fact that Peter was providing accurate details of the nature and character of these occurrences, their opinion remained unchanged. It was a grave error on the part of his Warsaw family members; one that Peter was unable to correct in the short run. Although he promised to restrict his discussion of the Nazi atrocities, he told himself that he would wait for a more advantageous opportunity, but he could not bring himself to deny that which he knew to be true. Peter realized that it was a challenge for decent people to accept that such savagery was within the capacity of human behavior. Regina, on the other hand, was a quiet young woman of twenty-one years at the time, who chose to keep her experiences and opinions to herself.

Peter had a strong respect for the truth. He believed being faithful to what he knew to be honest and accurate was an important principle. He also felt that no matter how unpleasant the truth may be, denying it would lead to lack of preparation for what might follow. In his mind, the evidence was clear, the Nazis penchant to believe that Jews were less than human was undeniable, and it would lead them to feel justified in wiping the Jews out of existence. However, Peter was most grateful for the shelter and acceptance provided to his sister and him by the Mandelbaums. So, he chose not to jeopardize their hospitality by insisting that they adopt his point of view.

He chose discretion as his tentative stance rather than force his direct perception of the German state of mind on his hosts. That evening, they enjoyed a modest family meal. Uncle Chaim, who joined the family for dinner, told some funny stories. Chaim possessed a clever sense of humor. Whenever George appeared ready to burst into tears, Uncle Chaim was able use his humorous side to turn George's tears to laughter.

***Uncle Chaim in Pre-war Warsaw***

Aunt Chaia Esther, George's mother, sat with them. She was an attractive
woman and quite tall. Peter had not previously made her acquaintance, but
he enjoyed being in her company. George was close to his mother. He
enjoyed her cooking of his daily meals and was especially fond of her
traditional holiday treats. At the table on the evening of Peter and Regina's
arrival, George's mother told them how, in the past, her husband, Elchanon,
expressed his gratitude for Peter's help. She remarked about the way in
which Peter reportedly helped his uncle to sell goods in Lublin by carrying
his heavy cases to lighten the load for him. It was true and Elchanon
confirmed his wife's recollection. Peter's mother, Ettle Fryszberg, had
directed him to do so because she knew her brother had two hernias and

wore steel spring braces for support. Elchanon also suffered with kidney stones and bladder problems. His schedule frequently required twenty hours of slave labor per day in the ghetto which was a severe challenge because of his physical condition.

George's mother cared for him, her only child, and tried to keep him healthy taking him to a local doctor for regular checkups before they were forced into the Ghetto. George recalls one occasion when he was waiting to enter the doctor's office while his mother was conversing with the physician. A man approached him and offered to repair his shoes. George removed the shoes and gave them to the man who took them with him. When his mother returned to take George in to the doctor, she asked pointedly, "Where are your shoes?" He told her that a nice man had taken them for repair. His mother, realizing George's shoes had been stolen, warned him against blind trust of others, given the level of desperation in the ghetto. He learned a lesson in trust from that experience.

The morning following their arrival Peter and Regina were determined to look for work to contribute to the family's welfare. Uncle Chaim found a sewing job for Regina almost immediately. Three days later, Peter found work in a sheet metal plant within the Schultz factory and near to Regina's place of employment. He could not work on a daily basis in the Schultz factory because he didn't possess documents that included his picture to serve as his permit for employment. Such documentation was necessary to avoid being unproductive and shipped out to the camps as a result. He realized that he had to secure a better work authorization document that included his picture alongside of the name of Peter Jablonski. Peter and Regina were interested in the opportunity to become useful members of their adopted family. Working made them feel as though they were making a worthwhile contribution in exchange for their acceptance and shelter.

The members of Peter's family were convinced that demonstrating one's usefulness even as a slave laborer was important for survival. Peter agreed and set out to obtain employment using the papers in his possession to enable him to fulfill his purpose. All members of the family had to present papers just to document their eligibility for slave labor. The companionship of family members was a true source of hope and fellowship for Peter and Regina. For the first time since their parents' death, they had people who cared for and guided them.

*Chaia Esther Mandelbaum*

*Elchanon Mandelbaum*

# Chapter Five

## Murder in the Warsaw Ghetto

*"Punishments: Any Jew who leaves the ghetto during the resettlement action, will be shot. Any Jew who acts against the resettlement will be shot. Any Jew who does not belong to the above-mentioned categories and is discovered after the resettlement action will be shot."*

*"The Warsaw Ghetto," Holocaust Education &*
*Archive Research Team*

One day in 1942, when George was just five years old, he accompanied his mother, his aunt Mindla Greenberg, and her son (name unknown) on an errand from their home at Nalewki 41. The moment they exited from their home into the adjacent courtyard, Nazi snipers began shooting indiscriminately using groups of Jewish residents for target practice. George could hear the successive blasts from the Nazi weapons. He watched in horror as three of his family members fell to the ground bleeding and writhing in pain. There was blood everywhere. His mother, his aunt Mindla, and her son were killed almost instantly. George was the only one who survived these senseless acts of murder, unharmed. Desperately, he removed his mother from the line of fire by dragging her lifeless body by her hair into a covered walkway near their home. The murders were a highly traumatic experience for a child of five years of age to endure, and one George would never forget.

He called for Regina. Upon hearing George's frightened screams, Regina tried to calm George before she ran to the Schultz Factory where her brother, Peter, and her Uncle Elchanon, George's father, were working to tell them about the horrific tragedy. When their shift ended, they both rushed home. Elchanon took George in his arms and tried to make him feel safe. The adult members of the family verified the death of George's mother, his aunt, and his cousin. With the aid of neighbors, Elchanon and Peter retrieved the bodies from the courtyard and arranged for their immediate and unceremonial burials. George would never be able to erase the image of his mother's murdered body from his mind. At his age his grief was exclusively focused on the death of his mother. Unfortunately, dead bodies in the streets of the ghetto had become a common sight, but they would always be uncommon for the family members of the victims

This event provoked shocked silence and unimaginable grief from family members and neighbors as they emerged from their various temporary locations to view the results of the slaughter. In that instant, an entire family was wrenched apart by one act of deliberate cruelty. George's father, as one can imagine, was quite distraught over his wife's murder.

Both Elchanon and Peter were disappointed when they did not observe the same level of anguish in Mindla Greenberg's husband, Szyja, over his wife's murder. Mindla was Elchanon's sister, so Elchanon was particularly disturbed by his brother-in-law's tepid reaction. Szyia's response was to get himself drunk. Elchanon barred him from the house. Peter and Regina had to calm Elchanon down. George cried throughout this disturbing ordeal. His mother's murder would remain indelibly imprinted on George's psyche for the rest of his life. "Even today at eighty-one years of age," George reports, "I can still hear those gunshots and see my mother fall by my side." Indeed, for them, the Warsaw ghetto had become a killing field. At age five, he watched as his mother's body was laid to rest.

The only remaining able-bodied family members in the household were young George and his father, Elchanon Mandelbaum, and his cousins Peter and Regina Fryszberg, and his uncle Szyja Greenberg. Uncle Chaim had moved to housing closer to his new job as a slave laborer in the Többens factory, another Nazi-sanctioned company located adjacent to the Stickerei Abteilung division run by Fritz Emil Schultz. Peter and his uncle Elchanon continued as slave laborers at the Schultz factory on Nowolipie 44 within the ghetto.

The Többens factory, like Oskar Schindler's operation, *** employed 15,000 Jews in the Warsaw Ghetto in lieu of their deportation. Employment there was a desirable alternative to relocation to the camps. Elchanon worked in the fur division at Schultz making fur accessories and wool sweaters for the German army to wear in the Russian winter. These clothes were required as preparation for the ill-advised German attack and siege at Stalingrad. The factories served dual purposes: on the one hand, Többens and Schultz were profiteers who provided goods and services to the Third Reich; on the other hand, they kept the hired Jewish slave laborers from the certain death of the concentration camps, at least temporarily.

A few days after the murders of George's family members, a neighbor who was sent to a death camp returned to Warsaw. He explained that he had been able to escape the camp because he was loading the accumulated clothing from the gassed victims into boxes on the train. Miraculously, he managed to hide among the clothing as the train made its return trip. When his experience was communicated, secondhand to Elchanon, he did not doubt the veracity of the man. Elchanon was gradually becoming convinced that the atrocities were real, and that he must take steps to protect his family from certain death. He began to put more credence in Peter's tales of the potential for liquidation at the hands of the Nazis. George obviously remained the most vulnerable member of the family, and he would require the consistent supervision of those remaining. Elchanon realized that

George, at his young age, must be protected, at all expense, from the possibility of torture and death.

George's father and cousin Peter began to explore the possibilities of releasing George from the dangers of the Warsaw Ghetto and they began to formulate a plan for liberating him.

*Courtyard entrance from street through a covered walkway with a ghetto building preserved Courtesy of George Mandelbaum 2001*

*Naewki St. where George's Mother, Aunt and Cousin were KilledPhoto from Life in the Old Country by Alter Kacyzne.*

*The Többens und Schultz & Company, a Nazi Germany textile conglomerate. [Wikipedia]*

*Remains of Original Buildings in the Warsaw Ghetto*
*Courtesy of George Mandelbaum 2001*

\*\*\* Oskar Schindler was a wealthy profiteer who used over 4 million marks of his own money to protect and save over 1,200 Jews by employing them in his factory in Krakow. He died penniless and asked to be buried in Israel where "his Jews" were.

# Chapter Six

## Survival

Family members frequently questioned Peter and Regina about their various encounters with the Nazis and their experiences with the threat of being captured. These inquiries were consistent, and they frequently became a subject of discussion late into the night. As conditions worsened, they became more and more obsessed with work as a necessary requirement for survival in the ghetto. Eventually, they would realize that even slave labor would only forestall the inevitable demise of family members. The Nazis often dragged people from their houses and shipped them to unfamiliar places in large numbers. Jewish workers flocked to the Többens and Schultz factories considering their employment there as a safe haven from German persecution. Jews who could, willingly paid large sums of money to work in the factories and avoid the death camps.

During these times, Elchanon Mandelbaum was isolated from his Gentile business partner, who continued to operate their precious metals business outside of the ghetto. They were able to affect some communication, but only on rare occasions. George's father fully expected that the effort to remove George from harm would depend upon accessing the shared profits from the inventory that he had accumulated with his Polish partner. Elchanon gradually became concerned with the potential for increased danger. Gradually, Peter was able to convince his uncle to attempt to smuggle young George out of the ghetto, lest he become a victim of the Nazi wrath which was particularly directed toward young children. Elchanon felt certain that there was enough equity in his business to pay for George's escape and reimburse others for his subsequent shelter. He was also confident that his partner would facilitate the appropriation of Elchanon's share of the finances, as necessary.

Peter worked in the transportation department of the Schultz factory division on Nowolipie 44, using his Peter Jablonski identification papers. There, he not only delivered manufactured goods to the trains, but he gained access to some useful information. For example, he learned that in the spring of 1942 the Germans planned to transfer their uniform manufacturing operation to a new location at the Trawniki concentration camp. That location would place the Schultz operation in a concentration camp rather than in the ghetto. The factory was to relocate approximately 25 miles southeast of Lublin.

In the autumn of 1941, the Germans had established an SS training center for concentration camp guards in Lublin. These so-called *Trawnikimänner* (Trawniki men) who were designated in German as *Hilfswillige*, aka *Hiwis* (willing helpers), were German nationals from Eastern Europe and anti-Communist and anti-Semitic Soviet POWs, especially Ukrainians, who volunteered to escape starvation and combat. John Demjanjuk and Jakiw Palij were both trainees at Trawniki. It was not until April 1988, that Demjanjuk would be found guilty as an accessory to the murder of 28,060 Jews while acting as a guard at Sobibor. Palij stood guard while 6,000 Jews were murdered at Trawniki in November 1943. He was found guilty in US District Court and deported from the United States.

The SS used the Trawniki trainees as assassins for several mass shootings of Jews or in anti-partisan combat with Polish nationals. The new location of the Schultz factory was a retooled warehouse building adjacent to the Trawniki labor camp. The factory would continue to manufacture uniforms, shoes. and other apparel to outfit the German army in the manner of the Schultz and Többins factories, established in Warsaw in 1941. The Germans relocated about 5,600 Jewish forced laborers and about 400 of their children from Warsaw in 1942. Elchanon was acquainted with a few of those transferees and Peter knew some of them. They were transferred to work at the reconstituted Schultz factory within the Trawniki labor camp at the end of 1942. Peter and his uncle continued to believe that working for the Germans was a necessary evil. However, before they were due to be transferred to Trawniki, and with the realization, that it would be too dangerous for George, a plot was evolved to arrange for his escape.

One day when Peter was at home with Elchanon, a man wearing a uniform that could be easily mistaken for that of a German soldier came to examine the gas meter and collect money for its use. Peter recognized the man's Polish dialect as similar to students in his high school classes, but his ability to distinguish different dialects or the man's origin based on his dialect was limited. Peter was interested in the meter man's explanation of putting coins in the meter to obtain gas for a limited amount of time without charge. That knowledge might eventually come in handy, he reasoned. After a short while, the man began to speak directly to Peter. Elchanon gave his nephew a signal to be quiet for the man would likely recognize that Peter's accent was not that of someone from Warsaw. Peter was speaking in the dialect of Lublin, which formal speakers of Polish considered slang. Elchanon did not believe the man was trustworthy. He feared his possible connection with the Nazis. The meter reader asked Peter, "Where are you from?" Peter realized that the meter man was interrogating him, and he was gripped with fear. In turn, he decided to return the challenge and asked the man in a harsh tone of voice, *"Are you from Gestapo 72 (a Division of the Gestapo stationed near Warsaw)?"* His retaliation with a similarly accusatory challenge caused the man to back down temporarily, even though he was not a member of the Gestapo.

Overcoming his reluctance to return the challenge, Peter directly asked the meter man about the nature of *his* role. In response, the man put his tools and all of his papers aside, then he looked at Peter, saying with raised voice, "You Polish citizens are wasting your time and your life. You should join with the fighters for freedom." The man's reference to freedom fighters encouraged Peter's faith in the loyalty of the meter reader. As he continued to speak, his words sounded more trustworthy. Peter replied that he was willing to join the freedom fighters, but he did not know how.

During the next two weeks, the meter reader came to visit and describe a plan for joining the freedom fighters to Peter but, Elchanon thought the meter man was setting a trap. His pseudonym was Felix, which was the name he used to obscure his identity from the Germans while working for the Underground. The specific information he shared with Peter made him seem above suspicion. However, Uncle Elchanon was not convinced of his honesty, and he counseled Peter not to trust him. They then lost contact with Felix for a few weeks.

When it came time to find a way to enable George to escape the conditions in Warsaw, Peter remembered that Felix had stated he had connections with the Underground, and he decided to seek Felix out for help. When Peter found him again, Felix agreed to help them by making a connection with Elchanon's Gentile partner to determine whether, or not, he would pay to protect George when he escaped from the ghetto. Peter knew that Felix, because of his meter reader role, was able to move freely outside the ghetto in the Aryan sector, where Elchanon's partner operated his precious metals store. They reasoned that payment for George's guardian(s) after he escaped would be critical to the success of any plan.

During his contact with Felix, Peter learned that his given name was Jan Szarkowski. Felix was the pseudonym he used for his relationship with the Underground. Jan agreed to join with Elchanon and Peter in a collaborative strategy to smuggle George out of the ghetto and ultimately avoid his incarceration in the Trawniki labor camp. In fact, if it was not for Jan's familiarity with the routines of the soldiers, the plan would not have been feasible. George's father still mistrusted Jan, but Peter argued that Jan was worthy of trust.

Elchanon was quite pessimistic when he encountered anyone who had seemed to gain the favor of the Nazis. He would wonder how that individual had attained his or her status, and whether he or she gained the position by dubious means. What might the person have to deliver to maintain the Nazi's good will? In other words, what might he or she "owe" to the Germans to earn and keep their loyalty? It turned out that Jan was eminently trustworthy. In fact, he was the one to give George his own identification papers so George could assume a new Polish name—Jan Szarkowski— Felix's real name. That false identity enabled George to flee to safety once he was safely removed from the confines of the ghetto.

Only Szarkowski's family, Peter, Elchanon, and George knew Jan Szarkowski's real identity; to everyone else he was Felix. He had no known last name. His German style–uniform afforded him access not generally permitted the average ghetto resident. In fact, unknown to the Germans, he was actually a member of the Polish Underground. Peter had a strong desire to join the group, an interest of which Jan was well aware. He could enroll Peter in the underground, he told him, with the understanding that no women would be permitted to join. Peter would have to separate from his sister. Although he longed to be part of the resistance, he would not abandon Regina, so he refused the invitation.

# Chapter Seven

## George's Escape from Warsaw

*"The torch of memory is precious. It can illuminate the world."*

—*Benjamin Meed, Holocaust survivor*

By mid-1942, the situation in Warsaw was becoming increasingly intolerable. More and more people were being relocated, or killed. Between July 22, 1942 and mid-September 1942 over 300,000 people were deported from the Warsaw ghetto. Over 250,000 of them were sent to the death camp at Treblinka. Finally, the tragic day came when the Germans threatened to take over the block of buildings that included the Mandelbaums' living quarters. Panic began to seize them as they realized there was a diminishing number of hiding places. Their capture and resettlement seemed inevitable due to the serious reduction in the number of suitable locations to shelter those in need.

Elchanon became convinced that the present location at Nalewki 41 had become extremely unsafe. The family began to seek a place to stay in the vicinity of the Warsaw Ghetto near the Stickerei Abteilung division run by Schultz, which spanned two square blocks. However, they were unable to find an alternative place of residence. Around this time, Elchanon's mother,

Grandmother Matla, died of natural causes, probably influenced by the stress of her situation. They prepared a funeral for her but, fearful of drawing the further attention of the Germans, they were reluctant to hold an appropriate, formal religious service.

Uncle Chaim's work assignment was changed to the Többens factory, the other family members continued to work in the Schultz factory compound on Nowolipie 44. Peter drove a big horse and wagon to ferry goods to and from the trains headed for the front. He also transported sacks of sugar, coal, and other products on the trip back to the stables. On the return trip, the wagon also hauled materials needed to supply the kitchen and the smaller facilities in the area of the factory. During these trips, a German soldier was typically stationed at the rear of the wagon to protect the merchandise and to ensure Peter's faithful attention to his task. There were usually three or four boys per wagon, accompanying Peter. Their job was to load and unload the work products at the factory and, then to offload them at the train station. On the way back, Peter and the boys were often able to salvage some of the food left in the wagon by the soldiers. These scraps helped to satisfy his family's perpetually unsatisfied appetites.

Peter learned how to handle the horses, outside and inside the stables. There were four wagons, several horses, and one truck garaged in this department. He tried to make himself as indispensable as he could. Regina, being the only remaining woman in the residence since her great aunt passed away, tended to the housework after completing her shift as a seamstress in Stickerei Abteilung (embroidery section) . His route to work at the Schultz factory required Peter to traverse two gated areas through the "large ghetto," and a densely populated area known as the "small ghetto." On the way to the train station, the wagon traversed along Zamenhofa St. to the side of the Umschlagplatz on Stawki, an area that separated the ghetto from the Aryan part of Warsaw. The Umschlagplatz was where Jews marked for deportation to the camps gathered in preparation for "relocation" before being loaded into cattle cars for transportation by rail to the camps. The quarters in those freight cars were so tight they would have no choice but to remain standing throughout their journey. The assignment to the transportation department provided Peter with access to the exterior of the camp on a consistent basis, and he was able to observe the plight of the dispossessed.

During the diminished housing situation, the Mandelbaums took in two local men as borders to help financially. Peter's sister, Regina, moved out to gain more privacy by living with three other girls from her seamstress' job at Stickerei Abteilung . During this time, Peter had many intimate conversations with his uncle Elchanon trying to convince him to allow George to escape, so that he might have the opportunity for adoption by a

Polish family. Even though he was only a child, George worked sweeping floors and packing boxes with uniforms in the Schultz factory. Doing so meant a few extra pieces of bread for his family and an alternative to the schooling from which he was prohibited. It also enabled him to emerge from the confinement of their living quarters while he remained under his father's oversight. However, this activity increased his exposure to the unpredictable brutality of the German troops. Despite all of the threats in his surroundings, for the most part George remained a happy, healthy, and playful boy. His father wished that he remain in that frame of mind. In addition, he was quite tall for his age, a factor that helped him gain access to factory work.

Peter suggested to his Uncle Elchanon that they reach out to Felix (Jan) to find out if he had any luck contacting Elchanon's partner. Enlchanon agreed, and they learned that he had reached Elchanon's Polish partner but he had hesitated to make contact with Elchanon because of his fear of Nazi surveillance. He informed Peter and his uncle that his partner agreed to finance George's escape. Peter convinced his uncle that George would remain a healthy child and would likely be adopted by a Polish family. Peter and Elchanon began in earnest to consider several possible plans to smuggle George out of the ghetto. In the meantime, they took turns looking after George while waiting for the opportune time to activate their plans. They dressed him, fed him, and accompanied him outside when they could identify safe places devoid of lurking Nazi storm troopers. Peter also reminded George of the procedures for "silent hiding" to keep him safe when the inevitable danger approached. This meant he could not speak, make noise, or leave the designated hiding place that Peter assigned. They practiced this form of self-protection together on a regular basis. George willingly complied with the routine, realizing its value for his safety.

George had a talent for drawing pictures, and each picture had a specific *dachu* (a hut with a roof drawn over the top). Peter enjoyed teaching George and encouraged him to improve his drawing skills. They were his signature talent, and before he developed more formal communication skills, the distinct drawings would make him readily identifiable to family members. One day, these skills would also serve as an important foundation for his architectural career. Peter also made primitive toys to keep George occupied throughout his restricted childhood. As George began to mature, he became inquisitive regarding his physical development and, as his father was dressing him, he often asked questions about his male organs. His physical stature caused him to mature earlier than the average boy his age. His father frequently shared a good-natured laugh with George over some of his more personal inquiries.

The outlook for small children was grim and quite risky in the ghetto. Since they were too young to engage in hard labor, the Nazis considered them expendable. The lack of wholesome food or necessary medication made it difficult for them to remain healthy. These circumstances made George's escape from the Warsaw Ghetto even more critical. The plot was planned and executed by Peter, Elchanon, Jan, and Jan's wife, Marila Szarkowski. They reasoned that Peter's job driving a horse and wagon for the Schultz factory division would enable him, as usual, to access the train station. Therefore, the route for the escape would be by rail, since Peter regularly drove the horse-drawn wagon to the railway station.

On this particular night in 1942, George was hidden in the large wooden box designed for storing feed for the horses and attached to the rear of the wagon. Peter had attached an enlarged the box so young George, despite his large frame, could fit inside. Several German soldiers who were responsible for overseeing the loading and unloading of the wagon were drinking heavily while on duty. The soldiers' drunken state would make the escape more feasible. Jan realized they had fortuitously chosen the opportune time to execute their plan.

Peter stopped his wagon, ostensibly to check the horses' hoofs and unload his bundles. As the goods were unloaded, Jan distracted the soldiers by engaging them in conversation. Meanwhile Peter managed to transfer George from the wooden box to an oversized, makeshift carriage steered by Jan's wife, Marila, whom they recruited for the task. Apparently, several heavy sewing machines had previously been loaded into the wooden box. George had to bite his lip to refrain from crying out because these heavy machines were constantly bumping against his long legs. As planned, Mrs. Szarkowski coaxed George from the box, wrapped him in a coat, removed the Star of David from his clothing, and placed him in the carriage in preparation for boarding the train. She filled the rest of the space in the carriage with rags. She accompanied young George by train to the Szarkowski's very impressive home in Danzig near the Baltic Sea. They concealed him in the basement of the house. George had never experienced such an impressive home. He would like to have stayed there longer.

When George first escaped, it took several sleepless nights before his father and Peter would learn that young George had successfully arrived at his new, comfortable location. They had mixed emotions—a sense of regret and a realization of the necessity for attempting the transfer, with the overriding realization that escape from Warsaw was in George's best interest. For six days, they heard nothing definite about George's location from Jan, who was their sole source of information. Finally, they heard the good news --- George was safely residing at Jan's sister's house for the last several days.

Jan told them this would be the arrangement until he could find someone interested and willing to take the child for a more extended period. He came to visit Elchanon and Peter every three weeks and brought drawings done by George with his distinctive *dachu*. This was the icon shaped like a hut with a roof over it that Peter encouraged George to practice for purposes just like this one. Jan also picked up a promissory note from Elchanon to give to his Gentile partner to guarantee the money for George's upkeep. His partner's name is unknown however, he continued to provide the needed financial support for George's well-being until George no longer required it. Jan turned out to be a most reliable associate who ensured that George received the best possible treatment.

Once they reached Jan's residence in Danzig , Jan Szarkowski designed the documents that would identify George by Jan's true name. From that day forward until the end of the war George would only respond to that name. The Szarkowskis cared for George; attending to his hygiene and providing him with nutrition and clean clothing for the several days that he remained with them. After staging George's escape, they also ensured his well-being. However, the Szarkowskis decided they could not incur the risk of housing this young Jewish lad on a continuous basis, lest they endanger themselves. Although, Elchanon's partner paid them generously for their role, they still feared possible repercussions from the Germans. A family that took on the responsibility of housing a Jew placed themselves in jeopardy of incurring the Nazi's wrath. The Nazis treated those who hid Jews as viciously as they treated the Jews. Nevertheless, in gratitude for their personal risks on his behalf, George continues, to this day, to refer to them as Uncle Jan and Aunt Marila. He kept a record of his ongoing communications from the Szarkowskis in a notebook with an attractive cover that they gave him when he left Poland. Their comments indicate their genuine concern for his ongoing safety.

*Jan and Marila Szarkowski's gift to George. From George Mandelbaum's personal collection.*

After his time at the Szarkowski home in Danzig, George was brought to

Warsaw to spend a few days in Jan's sister's apartment. This was during the Nazi's siege of 1943 and the bombardment of Warsaw which was aimed at

crushing the Resistance fighters. George next traveled with Jan's sister by cattle car to a work camp where the Germans released women and children with appropriate identification documents. The Germans regularly transported families from Warsaw to work camps by train. When the trains stopped to unload prisoners, the women and children were separated from the male prisoners who marched to the work camps. After they were released, Jan's sister took George to live with their widowed friend on a small farm in Oswiecim in the Carpathian Mountains. He would remain there for almost two years under her supervision

This was a location uncomfortably close to the Auschwitz and Birkenau death camps. George recalls the horrible odor which he later came to realize was the smell of burning flesh from the crematoria, an odor he cannot purge from his memories of that time. He also remembers his fear when Jan's sister and he occasionally encountered, the sneering German soldiers, rifles pointed and bayonets fixed asking for his identification papers as Jan Szarkowski. As they made their way to Oswiecim, all the while they could overhear the shelling of Warsaw during the Germans' second invasion and witness the devastation that was everywhere.

They hurried from the train station, fearing the Nazis would change their minds and detain *them*. They could hear the sounds of gunfire from the station area as they left. Most likely, the shots signaled the killing of the weakened or elderly prisoners who were exhausted from the train ride. Often the troops demanded sexual favors from some of the younger women and, if they refused, the women were killed on the spot. The screams of those victims became another of George's haunting remembrances that remain in his memory.

The Szarkowskis arranged for George to settle with the Polish woman who had lost her husband in the war, and whom they trusted to protect him. Jan's sister delivered the boy to the farm. The woman happened to be a devout Catholic and insisted on raising George in her religion. George was housed at the woman's farm in Oswiecem, just north of Krakow, for almost two years. He used the identification papers and related documents that identified him as Jan Szarkowski. The occupants of the farm seemed to be eagerly anticipating George's arrival. The farm included a barn and a chicken coop. There were a few hogs on the property and at least, as George recalls, one cow. The house was comprised of a large living area, but the dwelling had no electricity in it. It often grew very cold in the mountains, and there were frequent snowstorms. Therefore, the winter was often likely to be very cold. George was introduced to the woman's family as their cousin. He was taught to carry out a set of daily farm chores such as gathering eggs and milking the cow. He formed friendships with the two children who lived on a nearby farm. They soon became his neighbor/playmates.

During those two years, George trained himself to answer only to Jan Szarkowski. While he was housed on the farm, he attended Mass on Sundays and holydays of obligation. According to the woman, her deceased husband appeared to her one night in a dream. The apparition warned her to arrange for George's baptism if they expected to survive the war. Fearing his exposure if she took George to her church for this ritual, she took him to a nearby river and dunked him in its waters three times. During the third submersion, George concluded that she was trying to drown him, so he broke away from her grasp and swam underwater until he was a safe distance away from her. He swam to shore across the Vistula River, crossed a wooden bridge and paddled back to shore when it was safe to retrieve his clothes. When fully dressed he walked through the woods where he encountered members of an Underground Resistance cell who encouraged him to join them as a lookout. Uncertain he could trust these men he declined their offer, at first. Finally, he hiked back to the farmhouse of his hostess to reassure his guardian that he had survived, but he wanted no more Baptismal services.

German soldiers would frequently wander around the grounds of the farm as they waited to be assigned to the nearby battlegrounds. Elchanon and Jan warned George to be wary of what he said and did lest his identity be revealed. In particular, before he left Warsaw, his father warned him not to let anyone see him with his pants pulled down, revealing his circumcision. Conscious of his father's admonition, he avoided contact with the Germans and carefully monitored his speech when he was near them.

Later on when George met up with the Polish partisans again, he frequently served as their lookout and he was paid with welcome portions of food and vodka. He willingly performed menial tasks for them, feeling uncomfortable but considering these sojourns into the mountains as patriotic acts. The partisans were also engaged in a clandestine operation, brewing vodka from potatoes for their colleagues at a nearby farmhouse. They expected George to keep watch for the Germans while they engaged in the operation of their makeshift distillery. George monitored the movements and activities of the German soldiers and reported their movements for the partisans. While on his own or doing their bidding, he usually survived on no food except raw potatoes or scallions he found in the fields. Periodically, he would faithfully return to his guardian's farm to keep her somewhat apprised of his whereabouts. His guardian would express her displeasure over his escapades, but he would return to his watchdog role the following day. In hindsight, George presumed that Jan, being a partisan himself, may have known these fighters; provided them safe haven; and used them in his efforts to communicate with Elchanon, Peter, Elchanon's Gentile partner and other groups of Underground partisans.

*George wearing Partisan Cap; Partisan fighter in background*

George was proving to be a mischievous child disappearing frequently to associate with the partisans, and generally posing a disciplinary challenge to his guardian. However, when winter came to the area, the partisans moved to another location. Living on the farm became problematic for George and his host. He was unaware that by 1944 his cousin Peter was his only remaining family member in Poland . He stayed with the widow whom the

Szarkowskis designated until they were certain that the war had ended. When the Russians liberated Poland from the Nazis and overran Auschwitz, George began noticing Russian soldiers on the farm. One day, he wandered over to the adjacent farm and passed by a German soldier hiding under a wagon so the Russians would not discover him. The soldier signaled to George not to reveal his hiding place by placing his finger over his lips. George nodded in agreement, but as he walked on, he motioned to the Russians revealing the German's whereabouts. The German soldier was captured by the Russians and imprisoned in their POW area.

While George was living in Oswiecem, Elchanon had many concerns about the arrangements. He wondered whether the Germans would discover George in the farmhouse near the Carpathian Mountains where he was hidden. Did the host family expect George to work at slave-type labor in return for hiding him? The war could continue for many years. Would George be safe for all those years? Elchanon feared that he might not have enough money to pay for George's safekeeping over time. Eventually, Elchanon reasoned that, most likely the Nazis *"will not kill all the Jews before the war ends."* Hopefully, he believed, both George and he would survive. Elchanon became very skeptical now of all indefinite situations. He was even suspicious as to whether George actually sketched the drawings that Jan brought, or if they were imitations. Peter looked the drawings over carefully and once again he showed Elchanon the *dachu, or hut* with a roof that George always put in his drawings. He had to convince Elchanon that the drawings were, in fact, George's in order to provide him with some relief.

# Chapter Eight

## The Trawniki Labor Camp

*"The Polish Central Commission for German War Crimes estimated that the Nazis gassed a minimum of 1.65 million Jews—about one quarter of all those killed in the Holocaust—in three death camps."*
—*Richard Rashke, author of Escape from Sobibor*

By the spring of 1943, the Nazis ordered Fritz Schultz to move his factory from Nowolipie 44 to Trawniki within two months. He shipped the machinery and raw materials to the Trawniki labor camp, its new home. Finally, the Nazi hierarchy also decided to dispatch all able-bodied Jews as slave laborers to Trawniki. Peter and Elchanon knew they would probably be transferred to Trawniki with many of their fellow slave laborers. Anyone over the age of twelve was eligible for the slave labor camps. Jews who were capable of continuing to work might be sent there as part of the labor force. Previous workers and newly assigned prisoners were included as slave labor. They began to hear some news from the people who were the first transferees. It was encouraging—food was edible, everyone was able to have a job, and there was a hospital. People worked two shifts in the factory.

With these prospects encouraging his outlook, Elchanon delayed his escape into hiding. This would prove to be a serious mistake.

Elchanon Mandelbaum and his nephew Peter waited almost three months before being marched to the train that relocated them to Trawniki. In the interim, Peter continued to transport goods to the trains as usual. On several occasions, he had the opportunity to speak with some members of the Zydowska Organizacja Bojowa (ZOB), a Jewish combat organization. There was the hope that smaller cells of the group would assemble as an underground resistance force beyond the confines of the ghetto. To his surprise, Peter found two former neighbors, Cwi Zylerberg and Rozka Raizman from Lublin among the membership of this group. He remembered Cwi as the person who offered to save him from the DAW camp.

His former neighbors asked Peter to be a witness to the execution of a known turncoat named Eddie Malpa, who betrayed his own people to the Germans for smuggling food into the ghetto . Eddie chose to protect himself by revealing the names of people who were guilty of smuggling food to feed their families. Four young Resistance fighters spotted Malpa on Nowolipie where he worked. They captured him; took him into an alley; and, read the verdict for his crimes in a loud voice. One of the four drew a gun and pumped three bullets into Malpa's body. Peter served as their witness to the death sentence meted out by the four executioners. They then pinned the document with their verdict written on it to his lifeless body. After this sentence, there were no known additional leaks communicated to the Wehrmacht. Malpa's killing served as an example of the anticipated result for such traitorous behavior. Peter had observed a number of killings, but this one was unique in that it sent a message through the execution of a Jewish turncoat, who had chosen to be an informer on his own people. The killers apparently felt no remorse for killing Eddie Malpa. They saw it as a necessary step to avoid further betrayal.

Realizing the probable need to move to a different location with little advanced warning, Peter and Regina made several packages to secure their necessary belongings. When they had prepared their remaining possessions, they marched along Zamenhofa street in the heart of the ghetto. It was April 1943, the time of the Warsaw Ghetto uprising. Many Jews joined with the Polish Resistance in the uprising that extended from April 19 through May 16 lead by the Armia Krajowa (AK) fighters, the Home Army. The Russians massed along the Polish border were encouraging the Resistance's attacks against the Germans. They appreciated the rebels' efforts which had the effect of softening up the German Army as Russia waited patiently for *their* troops' opportunity to invade Poland.

Battles between the Resistance and the Nazis broke out in many locations throughout Warsaw, notably in the Central Ghetto and the main shopping area. Eventually, through direct combat with the partisans who were lacking sufficient ammunition and, the retaliation, capture, and torture of approximately 200,000 innocent residents, the Germans wore down the Polish Resistance. In fact, on occasion, the Germans would lash Resistance troops to their tanks as they used them to attack their Resistance fighter associates. During the uprising, captive employees were slowing their work output despite the constant yelling for increased rate of speed from the guards. To penalize the labor force, the Nazis brought in several oil tankers to fuel flamethrowers in the area, and they proceeded to burn many Polish homes shooting flames into windows and across roofs.

A group of partisans called Ghetto Defenders attempted their escape through underground sewer canals. The Germans struck at them using poisonous gas. During the last days of fighting most of them died in the final German attacks. The remaining members of the ZOB (the Jewish Combat Organization) committed suicide in a bunker in Warsaw rather than face merciless retribution from the Germans.

The ghetto residents recognized that the Nazis were committed to eliminating all Resistance fighters, and to severely punish the Jews. Meanwhile, the slave laborers were marched toward the trains for Trawniki, and no one among them was willing or able to generate any opposition. They realized that the armed Nazi guards would not hesitate to annihilate them, and they expected Trawniki to be an acceptable work camp. When they reached the cattle cars, they were tired and worried. The soldiers pushed and prodded them into the cars, and although many stumbled, most experienced only minor injuries.

The sliding doors of the train remained unlocked and were slightly ajar. Escape through the partially open doors appeared tempting, but lying in wait a short distance away were trigger-happy German soldiers serving as escorts. It would require very little incentive for them to mow down the slave laborers on board. Where could they make their escape? Most of them were unfamiliar with the location. Hungry, cold, and weary, they continued on the train ride until they finally arrived at Trawniki.

A huge and imposing double gate devoured the puffing train into the very center of the camp. A specially deputized group of locals brought the captives through the camp to show them where, with prior approval, they might draw water. Next, they escorted the prisoners to the barracks about 300 feet from the water site. This is where they would take up shelter for the immediate future. Peter and his sister, Regina, claimed a third-level upper bunk while their uncle Elchanon occupied the middle level bed just below them. They soon received instructions from the locals regarding job assignments, the nature of their tasks, and the work site to which they would report the following day.

The next morning, Regina reported to her familiar job as a seamstress. Uncle Elchanon and Peter were not deemed skillful enough for assignment as tradespeople. Therefore, they had to work outdoors laying railings for train tracks. Two soldiers supervised them from the vantage point of a Ukrainian school nearby. The technical specifications for laying the railings had to be precise. Oversight was the responsibility of an experienced local laborer who was familiar with railroad construction. He supervised operations at the train station to ensure accuracy as the tracks were laid.

After working for about seven to ten days, Peter learned that two of the camp's supervisors were from Lublin, and were previously assigned to the camp at Lipowa. They were selected for transfer to Trawniki to supervise the kind of work being carried on there, due to their expertise in railroad work. These men were actually Jewish prisoners of war pressed into service by the Germans. One of the two, named Shios, worked as a plumber and a metallurgist prior to the war. Peter was able to appeal to him to arrange a less strenuous job for his uncle. On the other hand, Peter was, by comparison, one of the stronger prisoners. He was assigned to hard labor, and he endured that assignment for a good while.

On one occasion, Shios's daughter brought a pot of food to the work site at noontime. The men usually worked right through lunch. After a while, supervisor Shios motioned to Peter pointing to the pot placed to the side of his work area. Making certain he avoided observation, Peter carefully lifted the pot from a kneeling position and consumed a goodly portion of the most delightful mix of meat with a helping of cooked potatoes. That meal, or anything like it, only passed his lips two more times during the next thirty days.

Peter and Regina benefitted from the fact that the Polish railroad supervisor lived in a modest house on the other side of the railroad tracks. Fortunately, for Peter, the supervisor appreciated the diligence and accuracy of his work. Peter, in turn, apprised the former Lublin resident about the heinous act that caused the demise of their parents. He also spoke of the tragedy that had befallen his Aunt, and his other members of his family at the hands of the Nazis. Shios, feeling a kinship with Peter met sporadically with him and Regina during the daytime and, regularly, in the evenings. They spoke about the supervisor's family and their past shared life experiences in Lublin. Mr. Shios also confided with Peter that he appreciated the work ethic demonstrated by Regina. Peter nurtured the acquaintance, because he realized the benefits it held in terms of more reasonable work assignments for Regina and him. It also resulted in better treatment in the form of an occasional home-cooked meal.

One day, the boiler operator for the commandant's building at the Trawniki Camp was found baking potatoes inside his shelter. He had stolen the potatoes from the kitchen and proceeded to bake them without realizing

that the odor would alert the guard. To make matters worse, the German

commandant's house, which was near the main gate, was adjacent to the

barracks where the potatoes were being prepared. The boiler operator's

punishment for the "crime" of baking potatoes was execution.

Unexpectedly, Mr. Shios was pressed into service as a replacement for the

baked potato criminal. He used his skills as a plumber to operate the boilers

on an interim basis. When his temporary status expired, he proposed to the

Nazis that Peter had the skill to assume the job and offered to train him. The

operation was not as smooth as Peter had originally expected, but it would

mean an increased portion of soup and bread which made it worth the effort.

He considered those items a proper reward for overcoming any fear of the

boilers that he may have harbored.

The commandant accepted Shios's recommendation, and Peter took on

the highly responsible position of boiler operator for Trawniki. Although he

had a good amount of anxiety about the responsibility, Peter soon

familiarized himself with the labyrinth of piping, the steam chamber,

adjustment of the water pressure, and the rest of the boilers' rather complex

functions. Since the boilers were coal-fired, another part of Peter's job was

to carry heavy supplies of coal from about 200 feet away to the boiler room.

He had to ensure a supply of hot water daily for showers to the commandant's quarters and hot water throughout the camp for the prisoner delousing process. These were very difficult tasks for a young man, but ones that brought worthwhile rewards of better treatment for Peter's sister, Regina, and for him, personally.

Peter decided to take steps to protect himself from the cold by establishing a permanent hiding place above the boiler room. There he would benefit from whatever ambient heat escaped from the boilers. *"If I am found to be hiding"*, he thought," *I will simply claim that I was repairing the pipes as part of my job."* Peter tied some rope to a chair and tied the other end of the rope to his belt. Then he pushed the wooden cover aside to enter the attic. With the chair in tow, he climbed over the joists toward the front wall of the barracks. There he placed the chair by the lone window. The location above the boiler room provided him with a vantage point to observe the many areas of the camp and the ongoing movements of the German troops. It also provided a goodly amount of warmth for Peter. He often ventured into the attic despite the fact that Mr. Shios warned him not to go up there where Shios had hidden "some personal items".

Uncle Elchanon was able to assist Peter on occasion. Because of his job maintaining the boilers, Peter could also provide visitors with warm water to drink. It was somewhat tasteless, but it fulfilled their need for hydration as necessary. Peter was able to wash his laundry occasionally. Each week, everyone in the camp had to report for delousing. In addition to sanitizing the camp's residents, the delousing procedure protected the goods shipped to the Nazi front lines from infestation with lice and other such undesirable creatures. Peter and Elchanon benefitted from extra showers and being able to delouse regularly, when Elchanon could sneak into the boiler room. The boiler room was a vital part of the camp's operation. Peter recruited an older man, who needed a task suited to his strength, to help him clear the wooden crates that were stored in the boiler room and cluttered the floor. He dismantled the crates so Peter could burn them in the furnace.

One time when he went to retrieve the coal from storage, Peter found a large pile of shoes removed from the murdered inhabitants of the camp. Most of them had the soles detached. He was able to take a few pairs, repair them, and distribute them to needy captives. While he was at it, he mended a pair of German boots for himself. The shoes were stored near the commandant's house, a dangerous location to frequent. The proximity to the commandant's office building made his travels to that area precarious and infrequent, but Peter reasoned that walking in rotted shoes could also be detrimental to his health.

The prospect of escape was constantly on the minds of Elchanon and his nephew. Yet, there was the danger that someone would hear their plans and report them. As Elchanon traveled outside the camp carrying large pipes to a nearby welding company, he encountered Jan Szarkowski, aka Felix, who encouraged him to try to escape and return to Warsaw. They went so far as to establish a tentative date for his departure. For the next three weeks, Elchanon had frequent conversations, absent Peter, with his brother-in-law Szyja Greenberg, regarding the plan. Szyja showed great interest in the prospect of escape. As the appointed day for the escape approached, Elchanon, for some reason, changed his mind and permitted Szyja to take his place and attempt the escape before him. Part of his reasoning was that he still did not fully trust Felix. Elchanon always thought it strange that Felix had no surname.

This turned out to be a serious mistake in judgment on Elchanon's part. He had expected that, if results were positive, his brother-in-law would report back to him, and he would escape next with Peter and Regina. However, he never heard from Szyja Greenberg again. Eventually, he learned that Szyja was killed in Warsaw in an unrelated incident. It turned out that it was Elchanon's final opportunity to escape from the mass murders that marked the last days of Trawniki.

Regina and her brother secretly began to discuss *their* desire to devise their *own* escape plan, but they did not want to be too rash in their actions. In the short term, they reasoned, there were many other obstacles to overcome. They needed to become acquainted with the camp and study the routines of their German captors. Peter needed to ensure that he could operate the boilers effectively. For now, it felt liberating just to be able to, privately consider the possibilities of life, and the hope of freedom. They had to be especially cautious with their conversations about escape. They could not be certain who was listening and whether or not people would spread rumors about any plans they might develop. For the present, they were safe for two reasons: first, they were producing useful goods for the German army, and second, they were serving as living proof of the Germans' propaganda that they did not kill the occupied people. For the time being, they decided to stay put. Unfortunately, their reasoning did not anticipate the Nazis' cruel intentions.

Very early in the morning on November 3, 1943, as he viewed the camp from above the boiler room, Peter noticed a large number of trucks accompanied by a squad of motorcycles assembling near the front gate. Military personnel spread around the barbed-wire fence and were headed toward the barracks by way of the front gate. From his window, Peter could see many people who were not fully dressed being dragged from their barracks. Others were ushered from the hospital sheds, with sheets over their heads. Peter wanted to warn Uncle Elchanon and Regina of the mounting danger, but he had no means of reaching them in a timely or safe manner. All the laborers and many others were marched to the fields adjoining the factory section of the Trawniki labor camp. Remote from Peter's view, the captives were forced to lie in trenches while they were assassinated in a mass execution. The rapid-fire of machine guns could be heard discharging on and off throughout the day above the blare of music the Nazis played to drown out the sound of the gunfire.

As evening approached, it was clear that no one had returned to the barracks. Peter came to the realization that a mass murder must have taken place and his Uncle Elchanon was likely among the victims, since Peter never saw him return to the barracks. The Germans labeled the operation *Aktion Erntefest* (Operation Harvest Festival). On November 3–4, 1943, more than 6,000 Jewish prisoners from Warsaw, including 400 children, and a total of 18,000 human beings were slaughtered as the Nazis abandoned the Trawniki labor camp. The prisoners had previously dug what they were told were anti-aircraft trenches. Now, they had entered the faux trenches only to be assassinated---the ditches became their graves. A labor camp became a death camp on that fateful day. In fact, during the period November 3–5, 1943, the Nazis murdered more than 25,000 Jews at the Trawniki, Powiatowa, and Majdanek camps. All across the Lublin district, approximately 43,000 victims became a part of the "final solution." It was the largest massacre of Jews in a brief space of time in the entirety of World War II. These actions were partially in response to the uprising at Majdanek where Jewish prisoners revolted and killed thirty-three Nazi guards, as well as, the escape of Jews at Sobibor accompanied by the killing of several Nazi officers. The Nazis decided that they would abandon the camps and liquidate the remaining Jewish prisoners.

Since no one came to take showers, Peter's boilers filled with steam. More trucks were coming into the camp. The commandant, accompanied by several troops, quickly opened the boiler room door yelling at Peter to get out—Peter followed his order while protesting, "Herr Commandant, I have to let the steam out because . . ." Before he could finish expressing his warning, the German officer turned and planted his boot firmly into Peter's groin and abruptly left the room. Peter got the commandant's message, but he also noticed there was not a direct order to depart from his location in the boiler room. Limping from the blow to his groin, he trudged to the boilers and ever so slowly began to release the steam to reduce the pressure. At twenty-three years of age, Peter, self-taught, was able to undertake the precarious task of releasing all of the built-up pressure to save the boilers from bursting—a job that he carried out deliberately and carefully over the next three days.

When Peter returned to the attic, he discovered a towel hanging near his secret location above the boiler. Wrapped inside the towel was a large chunk of lard wrapped in waxed paper and a leather wallet. Inside the wallet, there was a *Kennkarte* (Polish identification papers) with a picture of Shios. The name on the document was Leonard Strzalkowski, birthplace Lwow, 1917. He recalled Shios's admonition not to enter the attic, and now he could understand why. He realized the function of this secret location was to provide credentials and food for potential escapees. He pocketed the credentials contemplating their potential usefulness in the future. Mr. Shios had prepared his own documents anticipating the opportunity for freedom when it arrived.

For the following four days, Peter was able to survive with the gift of lard and water. The Germans swept through this barracks on two occasions. They seemed to be talking about removing the unnecessary boiler in preparation for abandoning the camp. It was November, and the boiler and its operator were both becoming colder and more endangered by the minute. Peter observed the camp's activities on a daily basis. There were workers coming into the buildings and the grounds to remove the remains of the people who were killed. The bodies of the murdered individuals were piled into the large open ditch with the others, where they were incinerated. The stench from the burning flesh was unbearable. Peter realized that his sister, Regina, must have been among the Trawniki victims since she, too, never returned to the barracks. Two of Peter's most precious family members were lost to him on that awful day. The people commandeered to clean up the remains of the victims were local Polish citizens. Many of them knew the

people who inhabited the lifeless bodies they now collected for burning.

Four days later, as the local Polish workers began to leave in small groups,

Peter decided to join them to try to make his escape

*A Part of the wall of the Trawniki labor camp. Courtesy of George Mandelbaum 2001*

*Chimney of the Schultz Factory inside Trawniki Camp*
*Courtesy of George Mandelbaum 2001*

*Commandant's House at Trawniki Camp – Courtesy of George Mandelbaum 2001*

# Chapter Nine

## Escape from Trawniki

*"Adjoining the coal storage was a big pile of shoes from the death camps. Most of them had ripped off soles"*          *-Peter Jablonski*

As he walked toward the front gate and out of Trawniki, Peter encountered a small horse-drawn wagon that was stuck in the mud. The driver was whipping the animal viciously demanding that he pull harder. Peter yelled to the farmer, *"Don't be hitting the horse!"* He could see the right rear wheel had settled into the mud. He asked, *"Do you need help?"*. The driver welcomed his offer and they both leaned into the submerged wagon wheel. With assistance from Peter's bony shoulder, the driver and he successfully pushed the vehicle from the mud. As the horse continued to pull the loosened wagon, Peter quietly positioned himself on the back of the wagon while the driver, unaware of his presence, pulled away. When the wagon approached the front gate, Peter turned his head away from the scrutiny of the German guard. The guard never demanded that the farmer stop the wagon. Peter had escaped from Trawniki!

In a short time, the wagon reached the road outside the camp. Peter jumped down from his perch on the rear of the wagon and proceeded to sprint away from the camp under his own power. In fact, he was the lone survivor of Trawniki; the only prisoner who lived to describe the events that occurred there. Now, he bore the identification papers of Leonard Strzalkowski; born in Lwow in 1917. Yet, neither of the pictures on his identification papers as Peter Jablonski or Leonard Strzalkowski bore Nachman's likeness. This was a dilemma yet to be addressed. Except for the German soldiers and the Polish conscripts, he was the lone witness to the horrific demise of the prisoners of Trawniki. Now, he had to turn his attention to avoiding the Russians as well as the Germans. It seemed as though each sniff of freedom brought the related scent of another threat to his survival.

Peter was concerned over his possible discovery by the *Hiwis*, the Ukrainian soldiers who were as merciless as the Nazis, so he walked quickly in the opposite direction from the camp. He took this route knowing also that it would bring him to the home of the railroad supervisor, Shios. After he explained how he had escaped from Trawniki and the loss of his uncle and sister, Shios's wife welcomed Peter into the house. She was quite friendly and prepared a welcome meal for him while awaiting the supervisor Shios' return home. She had much in common with Peter because they were both from the city of Lublin.

When Mr. Shios arrived home, he was surprised to see Peter and amazed that he had managed to escape the Trawniki slaughter. Peter immediately provided Mr. Shios with the identification papers for Leonard Strzalkowski which Shios had secreted in the attic of the boiler room. Shios was grateful for their return. Fortunately, for Peter, the Shios' home was distant from the camp and was overlooked during the murders. Shios had a shed near the house that was like a small barn. He told Peter that he could sleep there at his own risk. He warned him that the shed was frequently commandeered as a way station for German soldiers on their way to the front. Now that the Nazis were abandoning Trawniki, the likelihood of a stopover was heightened. The room in the shed was comprised of a double bunk bed with clean hay for sleeping. Peter was able to gain some rest in the comfort of the barn. He soon learned that his stay there would be for one night only.

In the morning, the supervisor directed his guest to the home of his cousin about four miles away. He felt they would both be safer if Peter used that as an alternative shelter. However, when he arrived at the address, no one was aware of anyone by the Shios family name. Apparently, Mr. Shios' cousin's family had abandoned that location. As he knocked on the door of each house in that area, Nachman uttered a brief Christian greeting (Probably *"Anghnredz"* meaning *May God bless you*). He had heard that expression offered by his Christian neighbors. Most people were friendly and offered some scraps of food, but they were reluctant to invite him to stay overnight. All the people Peter encountered had reservations about taking him in to stay with them. He wandered from place to place giving the false explanation, "I am looking for my father who escaped from Warsaw and is hiding in the local forests." Most people accepted his explanation, but residing with them remained problematic.

In a nearby village, Peter found an elderly Polish woman living alone in her family farmhouse. He recited his usual "Anghnredz" greeting to her. She was rather friendly. She told him that her son was in hiding a distance from the farmhouse. Ironically, she said he was hiding from Jews who tried to kill him because he told the Germans where a certain Jewish family was hiding. Although Peter was unsympathetic to her son's plight, he politely accepted her offer of domicile. In his mind, he drew a parallel of the son's situation with the Eddie Malpa shooting.

During that night, two men with guns knocked on Peter's door and ordered him to go outside the house. He stood up from his resting place on the floor. "Ah-ha, here you are!" one of them announced, as if he knew him. After a brief interrogation, they promised to come back and take Peter away with them the next day. He felt threatened by their vow to retrieve him. What would they do to him? Where would they take him? Their threat went unrealized. For some reason, they were unable or chose not to return for him. Peter suspected they were probably members of the Underground. However, he was afraid to stay at the farmhouse any longer. Word travels quickly through small villages, and one day he might be required to provide village officials a verification of his family origins. Given the inconsistency between his appearance and the picture on his credentials, he decided to continue his journey to another village.

A woman in this village, who was a former Lublin resident, recognized Peter immediately. After a short stay in her house, she told him that behind the building was her family's crypt. That night, he went there and found three boxes that appeared to be empty caskets. He made himself at home in one of those caskets for two nights while the woman provided a bowl of soup for his daily meal. The woman could not find any other accommodations where Peter might reside, and he found the crypt eerie and uncomfortable. It became obvious that his presence and possible discovery made her anxious. He had confronted similar anxieties among residents of several other villages. Rather than contribute to his former neighbor's anxiety, he decided to move on and leave her discomforting accommodations.

In one of the places where he sought rest, the proprietor asked for his identification papers. There, Peter had proudly told the contrived story of his father's plight and his search to find him. It turned out that the man Peter was addressing was the village bailiff and a former Polish military officer. He realized that Peter's photo did not match the ID. His son commented derisively, "He is a Jew!" The father put on an old Polish military coat, heavy boots, pulled out an old-type rifle from his cupboard, and said to Peter at gunpoint, "You are going with me to the police." Peter was feeling helpless—neither strong enough to run away, nor certain as to where he would go.

During the march to the police station, the village bailiff walked about 500 yards behind Peter with the rifle trained at his back. Peter shouted back to him, *"You were in the Polish army and so was my father . . . I speak German, and I will tell them that you were hiding me . . . Your village will despise you."* When the village bailiff contemplated Peter's threat, he decided that turning him into the police was not worth the possible personal implications for him and his family. He decided to lower his rifle and he yelled, "Do not come to us for shelter ever again." The village bailiff then turned on his heels to return home, leaving Peter to fend for himself.

On another night, after walking aimlessly through snowy roads with angry looking dogs barking intermittently at his heels, Peter came across an abandoned, dilapidated barn where he found shelter until the next morning. At dawn, he continued his trek until he reached his home city of Lublin. He hoped he would be able to find a hiding place in the house where he was born and where he played hide-and-seek as a young child in the basement and attic. On the way there, he stopped by the open market along his familiar route through the town and obtained a warm meal from a local grocer who recognized him. When he arrived at his former house, he realized that due to the war, it was not as familiar as he remembered it. The bombings had taken their toll and parts of his former home were hardly recognizable.

Continuing down the street, Peter stopped at the local barbershop, even though he could not afford the cost of a haircut. He noticed one of his former teachers, a man named Gromkiewicz, happened to be getting a haircut at the time. He greeted Peter as he entered the shop. After asking Peter a few questions about his circumstances, Gromkiewicz invited him to stay at his house while he tried to make other accommodations for him. He gave Peter some of his used clothing, which was far better than his current wardrobe of smelly, dirty clothes he had been wearing. Fortunately, they were a similar size. He also provided Peter with some food and hot water to wash himself. His former teacher permitted him to sleep at his house, while he arranged to stay at the house of a friend. The condition was that Peter had to vacate the house in the morning, and the door had to remain unlocked at night so it would appear that he had sneaked into the house on his own, and not with the permission of his former instructor.

In the morning, Gromkiewicz came back to his house explaining he had no luck making other arrangements for his former student. Peter decided to leave taking a different route out of Lublin. Occasionally, he saw some Nazi soldiers, but he managed to stay out of their line of sight. Shortly, he reached the main road and left the ruins of his former city. Outside of Lublin, he could see the dreaded Majdanek concentration camp and for a few moments he had thoughts of entering there and ending his suffering. Fortunately, sacrificing his own life was not something that he considered for very long.

As Peter walked past the dreaded camp, he heard a horse and wagon plodding along just behind him. The men reined in their horses and asked him where he was going. One of them asked, specifically, whether he was traveling to the village of Motycz. Needing the luxury of an alternate form of transportation, he promptly replied, *"Yes, sir!"* The driver then said, "So, jump in!" As they rode along, they talked to Peter about gifts he had bought for his family, since it was approaching Christmas time, and he assumed that Peter was a Christian. They spoke of other matters as well. As they neared Motycz, he instructed his passenger to give regards to his wealthy friend near the train station—a man named Zdun, who was a potter and stayed under a *pod blach* (sheet metal roof).

Peter did stop at the metal roof to give regards to Zdun as the driver had asked. As he hoped, emboldened by their mutual acquaintance, the wagon driver invited him to join them for a visit to the potter's home. The potter resided in a well-appointed family home of three rooms with fine furniture, a kitchen, and a large dining room with a substantial table. The family invited Peter to rest awhile and asked many questions about him and his father for whom he claimed to be searching. He answered most of their questions but offered convoluted responses when he felt uncomfortable or uncertain of the person's intent.

When Peter joined the family at their table for dinner, it was an awkward situation for him, being unfamiliar with the proper table manners or the songs that they sang celebrating the approaching Christmas season. Knowing or imitating the correct behaviors in a Christian family was not so simple for one raised Jewish. Peter hoped that this would be a good place to rest for a few days. The rumor was that the war would soon be over so remaining in this place and extending his days there as much as possible seemed like a good way to avoid confronting the Germans.

Zdun, who actually worked for the railroad, advised Peter to take the train from the station at Restiv to Berlin. The next morning, Zdun provided Peter with a train ticket to go as far as Warsaw. He claimed that he wanted Peter to be able to go "home for the holidays". Peter realized that this was

Zdun's not so subtle suggestion for him to depart. Apparently, the potter suspected Peter's true religious conviction. Zdun warned Peter that the train station at Restiv accommodated very few people so the train would not wait long for passengers to board. It would leave immediately.

Zdun escorted Peter directly to the train station. As they arrived at the station, the train had already begun to prepare for departure. Peter hesitated momentarily, and then he abruptly boarded the train. It was crowded with a number of Germans heading for Berlin. Fortunately, he could speak German. He was not sure how many stops the train would make and didn't know the safest place to get off. He was confused and tired from the many intricacies of his long and arduous journey. People began to talk to him as more passengers boarded the train. An elderly couple, farmers traveling to visit their son in Warsaw, engaged him in conversation. While they spoke, the farmer and his wife opened a box with a variety of foods, including some fruits, bread, and sausages. They willingly shared their bounty with Peter. This was an unexpected treat for him.

Peter anticipated returning to the area of the ghetto and finding only charred skeletons of its former structures. Reluctantly, he anticipated having to join others and hide out in the remains of once familiar houses. Since he was near Warsaw, he determined that he would try to find Felix, aka Jan Szarkowski, who had frequently urged him to join the Freedom Fighters. In

111

his present circumstances, without Regina, he was willing to become a member of the partisans. But he wondered how he would even find Jan. He decided to disembark at Warsaw and search for him instead of continuing to travel to Berlin.

Upon his arrival in Warsaw just before Christmas of 1943, Peter hailed a *riksza* (horse-drawn taxi) and asked the driver to take him to the gas company building where he remembered that Felix (Jan) worked. During the ride, he concocted another scheme. Since he was not shaved, had very little hair on his head, and was wearing his big boots and a working man's old leather coat with many patches, he decided to claim that he had escaped from a German jail in the town of Pawiak and had to deliver an important message to a comrade inside the gas company. He told the driver to drive fast for he was a member of the Underground fighters and had two hand grenades in his pockets. He avowed that he would use them, if necessary. The driver, in an effort to commiserate with his apparently well-armed passenger, indicated that his son also belonged to the Polish Underground.

When they arrived at the imposing gas company building, the pair approached the gate and spoke with the guard on duty. Peter gave the guard the same story of his escape from the Pawiak jail. He told him that he was looking for an associate named Felix whom he had reason to believe was employed by the gas company as a meter reader. "There is no Felix here," the guard answered, "but there was a Jan and a Bolek who were employed as meter readers." Peter then described Felix as being very thin and able to speak German. "Oh, you mean Jan Szarkowski," he recalled. Peter recalled that Jan used the name Felix only in his dealings with the Underground. *"Yes, yes,"* Peter said, and then asked, *"Do you know his address?"* "Oh, this I do not know," the guard replied, "but the Secretary is having a party on the first floor and he has the address list."

At this point, the driver began to become somewhat impatient, but he followed Peter to the first floor where they could hear loud voices and music. A very tall man answered Peter's knock on the door. In a nervous voice, Peter spoke loudly over the noise and explained, *"We have to rescue our comrade, Jan Szarkowski, but we have lost his address."* The *riksza* driver added, *"And I am in a hurry."* The men in the doorway tried to push them away, but Peter, using his foot as a doorstop, said, *"I have a grenade with me."* He made it clear that he was not reluctant to use it. Peter expected that his hand grenade bluff would make them realize that he was a desperate man. The men told the two of them to wait by the door while they left them and went inside the building. They returned with three other men. They looked menacingly at Peter and his driver, finally one of the three said, *"Daj im to* (Give it to them)." One of the three men gave the address to Peter. Peter and the driver were relieved. The driver admired Peter for his courage. He considered him a true hero for trying to reach Jan at the risk of his own safety. In Joseph Cambell's words, "A hero is someone who has given his life to something bigger than himself, or other than himself." Peter fit that definition. He was eager to find Jan to learn about the circumstances surrounding George's whereabouts. He was clearly George's hero.

Peter and the driver went directly to the address and found the building where Jan lived. The driver stayed with Peter even though he knew that he probably could not afford to pay the fare. Peter read through the roster of residents in the building and found a J. Szarkowski listed on the main floor. He mulled over what he might say when he found Jan and wondered if he would be welcomed or reported to the police? Was Elchanon accurate in thinking Szarkowski was not to be trusted? He knocked several times on the door. After he waited a bit longer, Jan answered the door, gun in hand. He looked skeptically at Peter. For a few seconds, Peter was at a loss for words as he kept his eyes on Jan's weapon. Finally, he uttered a question he had spoken to Jan in the past, *"Felix, can you send me to the forest to join the Freedom Fighters?"* Hearing that question convinced Felix only the Peter Jablonski he knew would recall his offer to join the Underground. Although Peter looked thin and ragged, he had to be the person Jan had worked with to arrange George Mandelbaum's escape. Jan asked Peter how he was able to find him. Peter briefly relayed the various encounters of that day's search.

Szarkowski paid the *riksza* driver on Peter's behalf, spoke quietly to his wife for a few seconds, and then, surprisingly, he left the house. Peter could not fathom what Szarkowski might have had on his mind. One minute he was listening to Peter's honest explanation of how he managed to find him, without asking many questions, and the next minute he bolted from the house. Why? Peter wondered, Is he going to turn me in to the authorities? Due to his many stressful dilemmas, trust was always the uppermost question in Peter's interactions with others. In that moment, like his uncle, he pondered whether or not he could trust the Szarkowskis.

Marila Szarkowski prepared some food for Peter, however the meal was accompanied with very little amiable conversation. She did ask how long Peter had been traveling alone. She was definitely preoccupied with learning whether or not anyone saw him entering the house. Peter chose not to mention the *riksza* driver to her, fearing that would arouse her suspicion. Just like many of the people he had encountered, Marila was concerned about the curiosity of her neighbors seeing unfamiliar guests coming into their house. Peter ate the food that the woman put in front of him. Yet he realized that if anyone asked him, he would not be able to identify exactly what he was eating. It was not a very appealing meal, however, he devoured it enthusiastically. He waited for a long time before he felt comfortable breaking the silence that existed between Marila Szarkowski and him. Her

115

demeanor reflected her discomfort with the danger that his intrusion presented for her family. He thanked her for the food; and only spoke again when Jan returned and asked him to follow. Peter immediately responded affirmatively and proceeded to do as requested.

Jan and Peter snaked their way through what seemed to be endless catacombs of small alleys, private gardens and, on occasion, some strangely quiet sections of narrow streets. Eventually, they arrived at a basement that housed a makeshift woodworking shop. Jan unlocked the door and he and Peter entered the isolated quarters. Once inside, Jan indicated that he had noticed that Peter was limping. Peter took off his boots so that Jan could treat his badly frostbitten toes, especially on the left foot. Jan showed Peter a bucket of water and explained how could use the water to relieve his frost-bitten toes.

After caring for Peter's foot, Jan initiated a serious and rather protracted talk about the rules for habitation in this basement residence. He warned Peter to be as quiet as possible and never to smoke while occupying the workshop. Finally, he invited Peter to use the shop as a hiding place and a source of woodworking activity to pass the time when no one else was nearby. Jan's genuine concern renewed Peter's confidence. After all, this was the same man who had given his cousin George the identification papers to safely assume his new identity as Jan Szarkowski.

Peter learned of George's whereabouts from Jan, and they discussed his return to Peter's care , his last remaining relative living in Poland. Jan explained that his first commitment was to protect George, but he was encountering a shortage of funds to ensure George's safety. The owner of the location where George hid expected reimbursement on a monthly basis. Uncle Elchanon's business partner was apparently unwilling, or unable, to add any more cash payments unless he received additional written communication assuring repayment. Another promissory note was necessary to ease his concern. Ultimately, Jan had hoped to find a family who was willing to adopt young George as their own child. However, the adoption had not yet materialized. On a separate note, Jan explained that this was not an opportune time for Peter to join the Freedom Fighters. They were undergoing significant changes within their ranks, and Peter's security would be in jeopardy if he joined at this time.

On his second day of hiding in the woodworking shop, Jan brought Peter a delicious soup laced with cooked meat. He informed Peter that he expected him to do some work to support himself while he was being sheltered. He was not the only person hidden in this location. Others required protection and their whereabouts needed to be kept secret. They consisted mainly of widows or single women whose husbands were missing and had not returned home from the war. These people were paying "rent" for their hiding places. It was very risky business.

Jan provided tools and personal support for Peter to carry out the tasks in which he was expected to engage. He did whatever he could to assist in the upkeep of the other fugitives and ease their circumstances. Jan asked him to make a hidden entrance beneath the basement coal storage bin for Mrs. Blaszczykowa. She was another Jewish fugitive, who was a single parent of two children, a son, Zygmunt, and a younger girl. It took Peter quite a while due to the many interruptions from the Nazi troops in the area and some other tasks that required his skills and attention. Meanwhile, Peter was waiting for an important adjustment to his *Kennkarte* (identification papers). He was waiting for his actual photograph to be attached to his identity card to complete his identification as Peter Jablonski.

On one disconcerting occasion during Peter's stay in the basement hiding place, two unfamiliar and suspicious men paid the apartment upstairs a visit. Peter happened to be working in the upstairs apartment at the time. The two men were very nicely dressed and were probably plainclothes SS officers. One of the local trusted neighbors made it clear that Peter should not engage them in any conversation for fear of revealing his true ethnicity. Shortly after they arrived, one of the women who inhabited the apartment discovered that a glass window in the kitchen was broken. When the SS pair left, she contacted a glazier who also happened to be a woman. The female glazier arrived to repair the window later that afternoon. About two hours after she left, there came a rhythmic kick to the door apparently made by one of the residents. This sound was a signal, a warning that they must all exit the building dressed as they were, without delay. They all did so immediately.

Peter walked up and down the street contemplating what went wrong. Along the way, he met Jan, who explained that the glazier noticed a very big pot cooking on the stove, so she reported it to the police. Jan confided, "We have our people there, too." He was referring to "Underground" infiltrators. The glazier told the police that she thought something suspicious was afoot in that apartment based on the oversized pots and other utensils for a normal-sized family. Jan told Peter that as a precaution, he would have to place him in a different hiding place. He took him to another basement apartment that had one large room with two windows and a curtain that divided the kitchen into two parts. He could only offer Peter a part of the basement residence in the building. Somewhat further down the hall on that lower level, there were lockers for the belongings of the people who lived upstairs. Later on, two additional Jews took shelter in this small apartment.

Jan's wife, Marila, came to visit Peter on occasion to bring him some cigarettes and the current military and political news. Once again, she reported, *"We have some problems with George. We have to relocate him from where he is to another temporary shelter."* Apparently, a part of the problem was the lack of money to satisfy George's caretaker in the current location since Jan had not received a recent payment from the late Uncle Elchanon's partner. In response, Peter told Marila Szarkowski that he had a watch that he inherited from his father who had received it from *his* grandfather. It remained in their family ever since. His father had counseled him, *"Someday, this watch may save your life."* His father gave the watch to Peter when they resettled in the Lublin ghetto. Peter kept it attached to his lower abdomen all these years. He told Jan's wife that it was the only item of value he could offer for George's protection. He promised her he would also look for a job to assist with payment for George's safe passage as soon as his revised documents arrived.

One evening when Peter had only been there a short time, Felix opened the door and introduced him to a young girl dressed in clothing like that of a farm girl. It was evident that Jan arranged for Peter to take up residence elsewhere. This young girl, Jan explained, would lead him to his new hiding place. Protecting him had become too much of a risk. The girl said to Peter, *"You will follow me, and stay three to four yards to the rear as if you do not know me. It will be quite a long distance. We will travel part of the way by streetcar. Here are your streetcar tickets."* Peter quickly got dressed to travel but could not put on his left shoe. That foot was still very swollen and painful. He took an old piece of paper and wrapped his foot in it to serve as a shoe. He noticed that Jan already was busily cleaning up the place to mask the fact that someone had been living there.

Eventually, Peter lost contact with Jan and Marila Szarkowski for a while. He never learned whether the gift of his family's watch was of any assistance to them. They did not say, nor did they request, additional payment. Peter's efforts to communicate with them any further failed. His Uncle's fond hope that his son, George, would be officially adopted occupied Peter's mind constantly. All that Elchanon ever wanted was for his son to be able to forget the past and resume a normal life. The family decided to send him away out of the necessity to secure his survival. Peter felt a strong commitment to make certain that his Uncle Elchanon's only remaining heir was saved. He expected to formulate plans to guarantee that George's escape would be permanent.

After a long, slow walk, Peter and his young female leader came to a streetcar. Upon entering the car, he remained standing to avoid engagement in conversation with the other passengers. It was the Christmas season, and most of the riders were women who had been shopping. When his guide disembarked from the streetcar, they were on the corner of Malczewskiego and Pulawska Streets. This was a big junction where streetcar transfers took place. He made certain to follow the girl as she exited the streetcar. She led him to a group of six to eight local people nearby who were waiting alongside a church wall. It was windy and snowing rather steadily. Peter stood among the group near the church while his eyes remained fixed on the girl, preparing to follow her when she began to move again.

Suddenly, someone pushed him from behind. When he looked back, there was a very large German soldier poking him with his rifle. He also noticed two more soldiers approaching him. He froze in place, numbed by fright. One of the soldiers started to inspect the package that Peter carried under his left arm. At that very moment, the awaited streetcar came to a halt within his view. He ran with all his power toward the streetcar, zig-zagging between pedestrians as he ran, and he jumped on board the streetcar. Women on the streetcar were making the sign of the cross and uttering prayers for his safety. However, he could no longer see his young female guide. He had lost her. He nearly panicked but got out at the next stop, just as abruptly as he had boarded. He walked briskly as if he knew where he was going. Fortunately, he soon spied the young female walking toward him. Rather than resume the journey aboard the streetcar, they walked a few long blocks until they came upon Malczewskiego 2. They walked through the garden and entered the building through the back door.Peter's "guide" tapped a signal he did not recognize on the door handle. A woman responded by opening the door from inside. He could hear her say, *"Oh! So, this is the man. Wait here. I have to walk my dog Lordzio."* Peter stood still as ordered not really understanding what to expect next. Meanwhile, he noticed that the young girl, who served as his guide, was running away. In a short while, the woman who had responded to his guide's knock reemerged from the apartment. She was dressed strangely, wearing two hats one on top of the other, two different color socks, and the aforementioned dog was leashed on a simple rope. *"My Lordzio likes good people,"* she proclaimed. *"He is kissing you. Now you will put on my husband's shoe."* She handed him a perfectly fitting shoe No doubt, she had noticed Peter's makeshift paper substitute for a left shoe.

They traveled along side streets while she sang a Polish song, and Peter walked a fair distance behind. The old woman, he later learned, was known as Crazy Michelina. As she led him through the streets to their final destination, Peter realized that she was not crazy at all. Her bizarre behavior was a means of diversion leading the Germans to believe her incapable of providing protection to those whom the Third Reich considered undesirable. Michelina Poacyliusz assisted different groups of fugitives seeking shelter in her area. She was sympathetic toward Jews, knowing they were counted among the Underground fighters who opposed the hated Nazis, and were victimized by them. Jan knew of her standing and felt she would take care of

Peter. Originally, Michelina had a vegetable stand that she transformed into a delicatessen on the corner of Malczewskiego and Pulawska streets. They arrived at the destination --- a relatively attractive three-room apartment with a kitchen, a washroom, and a small hallway. The apartment was inhabited by the widow of a military husband who had arranged for the arrival of several additional males. These men arrived shortly after Peter and were well-dressed. One of them was quite old; another suffered from tuberculosis. Michelina turned out to be a courageous protector of Jewish fugitives and other escapees from Nazi oppression.

While he was caring for his injured foot Nachman built a concealed shelter for her occupants while he stayed at the apartment Michelina found for him. Using the few tools he had available to him he constructed a double wall within a large cupboard All the while, he continued to treat his damaged left foot using various warm water remedies for frostbite. It took a bit longer to construct the wall than expected because he had to complete it when the area was as quiet as possible to avoid discovery by the Germans. He created several secure compartments within the existing structure. Fortunately, he had a good hiding place in the compartment while he worked. For building materials, he used spare planks that he found in the vicinity from buildings partially demolished after the bombings. Food was another problem for which Peter found a solution. In Michelina's storage closet, he discovered a bag with cut-off pieces of bread from sandwiches that she made for her customers. Previously, her routine was to take this bread to the family's farm to feed the livestock. Peter indicated to Michelina that he felt the higher priority was feeding of the human inhabitants of her building, she finally agreed to allow him to distribute this commodity as he saw fit. He began to use the pieces of bread to feed the human fugitives who were starving and find other sources of feed for the animals.

Michelina's son-in-law established a shoe repair shop across the street, where Peter would occasionally occupy his time and attention. Peter had an opportunity to apply the leather shoemaking and repairing skills he learned at Trawniki. He redistributed many of those pairs of shoes among the other prisoners and was always eager to apply the skills he learned to help other individuals. Under the circumstances, applying a recently learned skill was a welcome challenge. He trusted her son-in-law in part because he had his own problems because he was a Communist. (The Nazis viewed the Communists as another target group for annihilation.)

Peter finally did create an acceptable set of identification documents under the name, Peter Jablonski. He arranged to have a picture taken that he was able to attach to the ID papers. Now he was fully documented as a Polish, non-Jewish resident of his homeland, albeit by forgery.

# Chapter Ten

## Peter's Hiding Place

*"Together, we must fight . . . the evils of indifference, ignorance, injustice, and intolerance."*

—*Charlene Schiff, Holocaust survivor*

Several Jewish escapees had come to board with Michelina after the termination of the Warsaw ghetto uprising in May 1943. The new residents who arrived on Michelina's doorstep were people who desperately needed a place to live, a place that only she had the courage to provide. Michelina owned and operated a delicatessen at the corner of Malczewskiego 2 and Pulawska in the Molotow section of Warsaw. It was a small store with only four tiny tables, on the first floor of a three-story apartment building. Peter decided it would be a good location to transform into a hiding place for one group of fugitives. Next to the storage room in the rear, he structured a plywood wall with enough internal space to house four people. On the visible side, he attached dirty, distressed old pots and pans, and shoes to make it appear that this wall had been there a long while. This project was very risky for Nachman as the builder, and for the people who would pay to hide in his rough wooden structure. People with extra cash on hand were rare, but a small group paid to occupy the shelter. Their fees helped Michelina to survive and feed her residents, herself, and her husband.

Near the garden, there was a small wooden building covered in stucco where the caretaker once resided. When the Germans began bombing Warsaw in 1939, the caretaker had vacated the building. Beyond that house, there was a public toilet with running water. Peter dug through the floor of the caretaker's house to create a passageway and a hiding place within the public toilet. Set apart with wooden planks of various sizes and shapes, the underground shelter was three feet wide, six feet long, and three feet deep. Peter created a trip plate that opened and closed to enable access to the three steps into the hiding place from the caretaker's house. At the other end of the underground shelter, he placed plywood over the passageway that accessed the hiding place within the public toilet. (See: Peter's Drawing of the Underground Hiding Place on the following page)

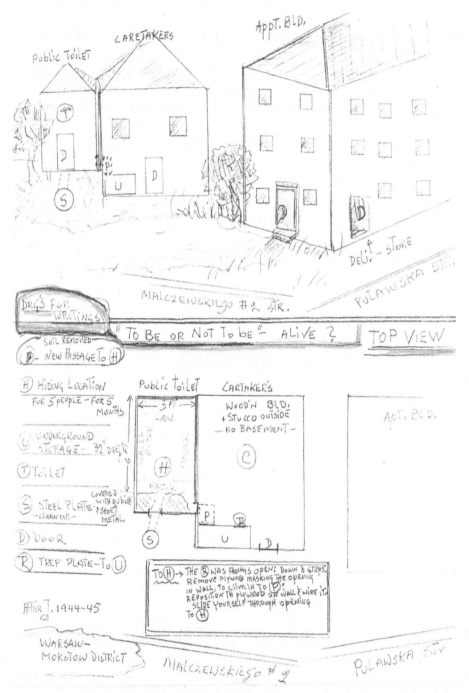

*Peter's Drawing of the Underground Hiding Place near Michelina's Delicatessen.*

128

To enter the hiding place after entering the caretaker's house (C), each person had to access the trip plate (R); walk down three steps to the underground storage area (U). Next one would remove the plywood(P) piece that hid the opening to the public toilet. Then you slid through the opening to access the public toilet and reattach the plywood to hide the passageway. This gains the person entry to the underground hiding place (H). Peter described his work simply in the following manner, *"I made an entrance into the sewer canal (S) to create a hiding place."* His construction of the space began in August 1944. Most of the work was done at night without electricity over a two- to three-week period. It was a big task, and Peter carried it out with skill and dedication.

Outside the public toilet and a few feet from the location of the underground shelter inside the caretaker's house was the sewage clean-out plate (S). Peter positioned pieces of sheet metal from bombed-out roofs over the sewer plate near the door of the toilet adjoining the underground shelter. Then he covered the sheet metal strips with debris from the recent bombings. If anyone approached the hiding place, the sheet metal rattled overhead, which would alert the people inside to restrict themselves to absolute silence. That building no longer exists in its previous form. Currently, there is a local police station on the site. However, it kept five people from harm from August 1944 to January 1945.

After constructing the hiding places and moving in its three boarders, Peter spent his nights foraging for food in bombed-out houses, garbage heaps, and especially, abandoned markets. He was the one who braved the dangers seeking food of any kind, and who took it upon himself to persist in searching for whatever sources he might discover. Each night, he ventured forth from the shelter on Malczewskiego and Pulawska in his search for food. He would often spend several hours foraging through abandoned buildings at great risk, yielding limited tangible results. On one occasion, he found a bag of rotten onions that fed him and his compatriots for three months. The odor of the rotten onions permeated the hiding place. Worse than rotten onions, was the odor of human waste, which Nachman removed from their shelter, nightly, to spread around and cover up on the grounds outside. This procedure protected the occupants of the hiding place from disease. and avoided their discovery by the Germans.

Each time Peter ventured from the hiding place, he covered his tracks to avoid any suspicion by the Nazis. To accomplish this, he walked on planks from the bombed buildings that he laid out to avoid leaving footsteps on the ground. This required him to pull in the boards when he returned. The planks also served as beds for the inhabitants at night. In snowy weather, he made certain that any tracks he made were cleared. He also had to be certain that he replaced the sheet metal and covered it with rubbish, dirt, and debris.

130

Peter contiually worried that the death of one of his rather feeble companions would cause an insoluble problem. The odor of a corpse and the machinations that would have been associated with its disposal would be especially overwhelming. Fortunately, he never had to confront that situation.

# Chapter Eleven

## Peter Meets Walter

*"Today we know what genocide is—we know where responsibility lies."*
*—Ruth B. Mandel, Holocaust survivor*

Peter had joined the Armia Ludowa (AL), the Polish partisans who were considered left wingers back in January 1944, using his official-looking documents with his actual picture and his pseudonym Piotr (Peter) Jablonski. Since he had blue eyes and spoke clear and fluent Polish, the resistance fighters didn't even ask if he was Jewish. He had been assigned to the Gannan warehouses in Warsaw with some military people from the Armia Krajowa (AK), the Home Army. During his involvement, he grabbed sacks of food to carry to the "safe zone" for distribution to the people who were encamped there. Other groups were digging tank holes to entrap the pursuing German tanks. It was beginning in September 1944 that Peter began living in his hiding place and caring for its inhabitants. The Germans resumed the steady bombardment of one house after another in the city of Warsaw. Some elderly people resided in the basement of the main building of Michelina's dwelling. The Jews who were in hiding were mostly men and a few women.

While Peter was on the move looking for food, seeking one secure hiding place after another, he encountered a thirteen-year-old boy named Wacek (Walter) Saltzberg. Walter was looking for a shelter from the Nazis and relief from the incessant bombings. He was born into an upper-middle-class family in Warsaw in 1931 and their apartment on Leszno St. nine years later was within the borders of the Warsaw Ghetto. He and his older brother, Jerzyk, were the children of Anna and Mauryce Zalcberg (Americanized as Saltzberg). Walter's parents and Jerzyk were able to obtain papers entitling them to work in the labor camps. Walter was too young to work, and his parents were not permitted to keep him with them, so they were forced to abandon him to survive on his own. He last saw his parents and his brother in the spring 1942. Presumably, they became victims of the Nazi death camps.

Fortunately, Walter encountered a family friend and a member of the Polish Underground, Dr. Kazimierz Wieckowski, a Christian physician, who smuggled Walter out of the Warsaw Ghetto. Dr Wieckowski hid the eleven year old in his own apartment for two years. When anyone entered the apartment, Walter immediately rushed into the bathroom and hid between the bathtub and the wall. He had no access to books, radio, or television during those years. During the Warsaw Uprising, Dr. Wieckowski's house was bombed and Walter had to abandon his relatively safe accommodation. He fled to a nearby building. There he found other Jews in hiding, including Peter who was older by 10 years.

Shortly after his arrival in this new shelter bombs struck the building and only he and Peter remained alive. Walter just barely managed to survive. Buried up to his neck in rubble from the bombing, he suffered a very bad laceration and a severely broken leg. Despite his own head injury incurred during the same bombing, Peter found the teenager amid the heavy debris and extracted Walter from the rubble. He treated the wounds as best he could. Walter's leg obviously required treatment beyond Peter's ability to provide. Ignoring his own injuries, Peter carried Walter to his underground shelter. Realizing the danger of infection and gangrene, Peter cut off the bottom of his shirt and soaked it with his own urine to disinfect the open wounds on Walter's leg. They had no water and would have had to go out at night and travel to the nearest ground pump to obtain water. Peter knew that such an excursion would be far too risky. He prepared food for Walter, and, eventually, he was able to take Walter to an orphanage where he was treated by a Russian doctor.

Peter and Walter occupied the hiding place with three older men who were Peter's original tenants --- Ludwig, Stasiek, and Kazik. Peter was the

134

only refugee young and healthy enough among the five to go out at night and search for food. Kazik was overweight and old. Stasiek was more than seventy years old and sick with tuberculosis; Ludwig, the oldest of the group, was severely overweight and moved in and out of the passageway with great difficulty; Walter had a severely broken leg, and finally there was Peter. The old men were not happy to accept Walter fearing his cries of pain would give them away. One night, Peter found a few bottles of preserved tomatoes and some sorrel in a basement nearby. With rockets illuminating the night sky and military patrols in the area, it took Peter two hours to get back to the shelter, crawling on all-fours all the way. Upon his return, he found Stasiek. choking Walter to stop him from crying out in pain. Stasiek was afraid that Walter's painful cries would alert the German patrols and draw them to the shelter. On the other hand, Walter was in excruciating pain and could not even straighten his broken leg. Peter pushed Stasiek away threatening, *"From now on you will go for your own food."* The inhabitants knew they could not find their own food, since they could hardly crawl into the shelter alone. Peter's threat calmed them down and Walter was safe again. As problematic as Walter's loud cries had become, Peter would not allow the others to turn on him. Peter observed, *"A healthy person cannot believe another person is sick."*

They slept on four assigned planks: one each for Kazik, Stasiek, and Ludwig. Peter shared a plank with Walter who could only lie flat on his back. Furthermore, Peter took the teenager to the toilet whenever necessary and possible. Since their sleeping quarters was completely dark, Peter poked a hole through the edge of the material covering the circular trip plate so that a ray of light could guide them at night. After a while, the shelter occupants became disoriented as to the days of the week and the length of time of their concealment. Over the five months, each occupant wore one set of clothes and never removed his shoes.

Hunger was taking its toll, and that contributed to their confusion. Peter reported, *"We were short of bread after about ten days."* Peter had to risk seeking new sources of food on unfamiliar streets. On a street in back of the garden, he found a few jars of fruit preserves. He knew these would not last too long and he realized their need for water. Therefore, he devised a collection system for gathering rainwater. In a pinch, he would also draw water from the boiler in the caretaker's house. As days were beginning to become colder, he collected whatever he could to keep the inhabitants of the shelter warm, especially at night. *"I collected more 'junk' to cover us, so that this would not be a problem"*, he wrote.

Another problem arose when snow began to fall and stuck on the ground for several days. Because he was traveling much farther away to find food and beyond the planks near the shelter, Peter worried about leaving footprints in the snow. He covered his shoes with rags so they would not make clear impressions. *"I had a few long planks which I used to make a walk positioning it over the rubbish, not to have marks of foot-prints."* Resourcefulness permeated Peter's every action. On one occasion, a German soldier entered the caretaker's house, but he did not discover the group hiding there. The planks were kept inside the shelter, which took up some of their precious space. Soon all of the nearby buildings were devoid of any food. One night, Peter actually stole food from the Germans. He absconded with sacks of potatoes, rutabagas, onions, and cabbages, which would provide a number of meals. Many years after the war, during a videotaped interview with a neighbor in Canada, Peter was asked, *"How did you manage to steal all of that food?"* He responded, *"I did not steal anything."* The interviewer persisted, *"But you got those things to eat." "Yes,"* he replied with a wry smile. *"But I did not steal anything."*

Peter came up with another idea to ensure the ongoing safety of the group. He had consistently anticipated the Russian offensive against the German forces. It was his expectation that the Russians might be more intent on killing Nazis than Jews. He managed to climb to the fifth floor of the empty skeleton of a bombed-out building nearby to observe the activity of the Germans as they prepared to defend against the Russian advance. The two countries had divided Poland with the Russians taking the eastern half, while leaving the west to the Germans. Peter expected the Russians would not be satisfied with only a part of the country. On one particular night and most of the next, in freezing temperatures, he lay flat on the roof observing German patrols passing by in groups of three or more, some large trucks, and small groups of Polish workers marched on the same road. When he returned late the next day, he saw an occasional war plane accompanied by light flares and rockets at night, but no sign of Russian troops. Apparently, the Russians were biding their time. *"No Russians yet."*, he reported disappointedly to his comrades.

That evening when Peter returned to the bunker, a dog was barking directly above the sewer plate near the door to the public toilet. Since the Germans tended to kill animals that did not belong to them, Peter reasoned that this must be a German-owned dog and that German troops would likely be nearby. At first, he waited until the dog stopped barking. The Germans paid it no heed. However, every few days it reappeared and resumed barking. Finally, the barking became weaker and weaker. Peter decided it was not a German police dog. He opted to go out and confront the dog. It was hungry, homeless, apparently abandoned, and barely surviving. Peter was concerned that if the dog belonged to the Germans, its barking would possibly bring them too close to their hiding place. *"He was homeless and hungry just like we were.*", Peter concluded. So he picked up the animal, carried it to a different location, and made certain it could not find its way back.

Food was a constant concern for the inhabitants of the shelter. Peter moved slowly and very carefully from house to house hoping to find something to eat. He tried to avoid the persistent flares fired by the Germans. On one occasion, he discovered a few sacks of rotten onions and some rutabagas. He apportioned the food into smaller packages and hid the packages in a half-demolished house to keep them from other Polish scavengers. He constantly prepared for the future, anticipating problems. Despite his own fatigue and the threat of German intervention, Peter made three trips that night, finding more onions and rutabagas in the process. He felt it necessary to retrieve all of the food before it was discovered by other search parties. Hopefully, he and the other four in the shelter would have enough food to survive the winter.

That winter, several conditions brought an increase of discomfort to the bunker's inhabitants. Stasiek, who had tuberculosis, began coughing frequently, which posed another threat of discovery. All the people in the shelter were infested with lice. The bites caused severe itching and bleeding. After being confined to the bunker for four months, wearing the same dirty, fetid clothing, they began to resent one another. They lacked an adequate

139

water supply and without water, they could not cook. There was snow but not enough to collect and melt for water. And they lacked a usable heat source. They were becoming extremely weak and more and more dependent upon Peter's ingenuity.

Peter decided to use his pocketknife to cut holes in the bottom of an aluminum pot. He then created a makeshift stove with three bricks and heated it by igniting a wood fire within the bricks. He positioned the stove between the walls of their small building and the adjoining public toilet. The roof was open, so the smoke was able to escape. However, he could only use this device on a windy and cloudy day when the Nazis could not detect the escaping smoke or smell the cooking meal. Even then, he was taking a chance. But at this point, either way, survival was in jeopardy. So, the refugees often dined solely on rotten onions and rutabagas. Meager though it was, the food had a satisfying effect on their appetites. Ludwig, who had studied in Paris where he had frequented quite a few comedy shows, lifted everyone's spirits by telling jokes and humorous stories, as they devoured their limited food supply.

One day after eating, the refugees heard heavy steps on top of the sheet metal covering the sewer plate. They could hear German spoken above, a woman was talking half in German and half in Polish. It was, unmistakably, Michelina. She and her husband, Anton, were the only ones who knew the exact location of their secret hiding place. *"We became frozen stiff!"*, exclaimed Peter. Evidently when Michelina broke away from a group walking in the street, a German soldier became suspicious and followed her. "Mein Katzen, Mein Katzen (My cats, my cats)," she screamed. The Germans could be heard saying, "Verrückt, verrückt (Crazy, crazy)," as they walked away from her. The concealed group became rigid with fear, reluctant to make the slightest noise. They could hear more talking, but it gradually faded away, indicating that the speakers left the area. Peter recognized Michelina's voice. However, he decided not to venture outside for two days because he believed the location was under observation. Finally, he slowly put his head outside, looked around, and spied several large chunks of bread in the snow. Near the floor of the entrance to the bunker, he noticed a big brown kerchief with a large chunk of sausage wrapped in it. He hastily retrieved it, overjoyed by the discovery of this generous bounty.

The other people in the shelter could not believe their eyes when Peter showed them the sausage. It was a long time since a piece of edible meat entered their mouths. Peter divided the sausage evenly among them, and they enthusiastically devoured the feast that evening, including that rare, welcome piece of meat. It seemed that Michelina had convinced the Germans that the food was for her cats, and then wrapped it in her neckerchief, which she threw on the ground for Peter and the refugees. Soon afterward, they realized that they had to ration the food supply more sparingly . By now, they had spent five difficult months hiding in a very tight space. As Peter reflected later on those five months, he could not imagine that they managed to survive, but survive they did.

Given the proximity of the Soviet troops who could be seen from the rooftop in a suburb across the Vistula River from Warsaw, the hidden Jews did not know what to expect next. Panic began to set in. Peter discovered an order that was posted on the streets by the German High Command demanding, "*All people must vacate the city.*" Peter understood this declaration to mean that only military personnel would be permitted in the city. Now the occupants of Peter's hiding place were in a real dilemma. It appeared that the war was approaching an end, yet all hope for relief from hiding was dwindling due to the Germans' last ditch efforts at destroying Warsaw.

The five survivors decided to abandon their tiny shelter in January, 1945. The Ghetto residents who had survived the bombings were proceeding to the small town of Pruszkow, eleven miles from Warsaw. If they were discovered, they would certainly be denounced there as *Juden*. The streets of Warsaw were crowded with people carrying their limited belongings on their way to Pruszkow. The evacuees recognized the urgency to proceed quickly for the Russians would be probably be in Warsaw in the coming days. At that same time, German planes continued to fly over the city dropping bombs as a reprisal for the Warsaw Uprising. When the bombing subsided Ludwig, Stasiek, and Kazik set out to find the whereabouts of family and friends who they expected to be sheltered in various areas of Warsaw.

For the next few nights, Peter and Walter could hear the heavy tanks entering the main street. Because this area was designated as a military zone; no one was considered a civilian. Only combatants were permitted to occupy the zone where Peter and Walter were located. Therefore, anyone found occupying that area was fair game as a military target. Occasionally, planes of the Luftwaffe flew over and strafed the city. Rockets and flares were lighting up the evening sky, however, no Russians were to be found. These occurrences are some examples of the events in the lives of a people who had the will and the good fortune to overcome the intolerable and live to tell about it. Their circumstances defied a reasonable explanation. It is difficult to offer a meaningful rationale for the odious events they endured during those five long months in hiding.

# Chapter Twelve

## The Final Struggles

*"You must take history with its beauty and you must take it with its degradation. You've got to deal with it for us to be whole human beings and to make a difference."*

*—Leon Bass, World War II veteran and educator*

The Warsaw Uprising ended on May 16, 1943. In the months that followed, the Soviet Union kept their troops from entering the city of Warsaw. They stood idly by as the Germans killed the Poles in the streets or in concentration camps. In January 1945, the Russian offensive began. Soviet troops entered Warsaw on January 17 and eventually found Peter's cluster of despondent refugees and confronted them in their hiding place. With machine guns pointed at their faces, the inhabitants of the shelter were accused of being German spies. Fortunately, Ludwig spoke Russian fluently and explained their circumstances to the Russians' satisfaction. Instead of treating them as adversaries, the Russian soldiers fed them hot food and lots of bread. As Peter expressed the end of their long underground existence,

*"My comrades came out from [the] bunker. They had somebody in Warsaw, and I was left with an invalid, [with]nowhere to go."* When his colleagues emerged from the bunker, their appetites were satisfied and their anxieties were lowered. Peter remained to care for the injured Walter, since there was no remaining members of Walter's family. He had nowhere to go for food or shelter and Peter realized that thirteen-year-old Walter was in constant pain.

Three days later, Michelina and her husband, Anton Poacyliusz, found Peter and Walter. They led the two refugees to a safer locale, where they took up residence in an empty, bombed-out apartment with only two of its four walls still standing. As advised, they hid in the basement of the building near a staircase with Michelina and Anton, Richard, his wife and daughter, Halina from Warsaw, Dr. Stefa Swieca, Szyja-Kazimierz, Szalewski, and a few other women. They merged together under a stairwell to form hiding places squeezing among each other's bodies to avoid being seen as they anticipated the Russians continued arrival. They were spared along with several Poles who hid in other parts of the building with the Jewish refugees and other non-Jewish dwellers. They did not feel hopeless as Michelina had supplied them with bread and water. Peter made a box-like room inside to keep Walter warm. At the time, Walter had to use a chair with wheels to propel himself around the area. Peter went out to the streets to gather pieces of wood that he bundled for sale to any available buyers remaining in the

Praga section of Warsaw. He used the money to buy food for Walter and himself. Peter wrote, *"Gradually, I found connections to the Jewish Congress. With many difficulties I accomplished to take Wacek (Walter) to Otwock [Poland] Orphanage. Myself I turned sick, headaches!"*

In spring 1945, Peter began to suffer with a serious illness accompanied by his severe headaches. Despite his weakened condition, he was approached by the Pneyliusz family who were in need of repairs to their home. They had lost their only child, a fourteen-year-old son. Peter found it very difficult to ignore the hardship of others despite his own physical debilitation. However, due to his failing health, he found the renovation too challenging for him, physically. Peter was the type of person who could not ignore the plight of another family in need, particularly one that had shared the experience of German oppression during the war. Perhaps they reminded him of the once close family he had and lost due to Nazi brutality during the war. How he missed his parents and his sister, Regina. Somehow, their circumstances did not make him resentful, but more responsive to victims whose families experienced similar loss. However, due to his own ill health, he had to discontinue this particular project.

# Chapter Thirteen

## Peter and Sabina: Life after the War

*"I grasped the meaning of the greatest secret that human poetry and human thought and belief have to impart: The salvation of man is through love and in love. I understood how a man who has nothing left in this world still may know bliss, be it only for a brief moment, in the contemplation of his beloved."*

—*Viktor Frankl, Holocaust survivor*

Sabina Myszkowski was born on October 27, 1921 in Wilno, Poland. She was the sixth of eight children. Sabina left home at 18 years of age and traveled more than a hundred miles to Warsaw from near the Russian border. She moved into an apartment in Warsaw. Her sister Helen joined her in her apartment two years later. Soon after, Helen was captured by the Nazis and was forced to make parachutes in a slave labor camp. When the war was over she had been moved to a refugee camp in Germany. From there she immigrated to Canada in October 1945.

Sabina had no way of contacting her sister or knowing her whereabouts. Rather than remain alone in the apartment, she invited two older women to stay with her and share the rent. Sabina found work in a grocery store and lived a meager existence. The older women had little in common with Sabina and decided to move to another location. After they left, Sabina was fortunate to gain employment at the local post office. This job provided her with a higher salary so she was able to sustain the increased rental burden when the women moved out of the apartment. She invited another young woman, one of her coworkers, to live with her to make her living expenses more bearable.

It turned out that the manager of the post office, a married man, took advantage of Sabina's roommate and impregnated her. When he realized the young woman was pregnant, he would come to their apartment uninvited to bring them food as a way of easing his own guilt. At his insistence, Sabina's companion agreed to undergo an illicit abortion. The abortion, performed under questionable surgical conditions, caused the young woman to become infected and she nearly died. In the closing months of the war in Europe in 1945, Peter went to the post office in Warsaw to search for addresses of his family and friends and was helped by Sabina. He was so impressed with her beauty and personality that he made the decision to pursue a relationship with her. Evidently, she was accepting of his advances. It was love at first sight. Peter was devoted to Sabina from their first meeting. That devotion continued for the rest of their lives.

*Sabina as Peter First met Her in Warsaw*

Neither Sabina nor her roommate trusted the post office manager. Peter would often escort Sabina home from work and stay at the apartment to discourage the Post Office manager's visits.. These were dangerous times for a young woman to travel the city alone without an escort especially because the Russians were unpredictable. Peter and Sabina soon began to date on a regular basis. When he described his war-time experiences to Sabina, she was very empathic. Although they both had very little financial resources, Sabina pledged to help him secure protection for his cousin,

George. When the war ended, they found an apartment with a small terrace in Warsaw, on Targowa Street in the Praga section, where they lived together. Peter was able to land a job with the American Joint Distribution Committee. He recommended people who needed help and delivered food to each family once per month.

*Peter in Post-War Warsaw*

After they settled into the apartment in Warsaw, Peter immediately began to make plans for his cousin George to join them. He first contacted the Szarkowskis. At his request, Marila Szarkowski traveled to the farmhouse where George had been staying at Oswiecim in the Carpathian Mountains to escort him back to Warsaw to his cousin's care. She advised George that it would be in his best interest to leave that hiding place and come with her to Warsaw to reunite with Peter. He resisted at first, and when he continued to resist, she announced in no uncertain terms, "WE ARE GOING!" Finally, he relented and boarded the train with her. He used his official-looking documentation as Jan Szarkowski to safely accompany her. Marila climbed aboard the train tightly clasping George's hand, and they traveled to the railroad hub at the city of Krakow. From Krakow, the two of them boarded a train to Warsaw so Jan's wife could deliver George safely to Peter.

*George Returned to Warsaw Marila Szarkowski, George, and Peter*

George resented his removal from a place where he felt safe most of the time. He was not comfortable living with Peter and Sabina when he first arrived at their apartment. George did not appreciate being uprooted again, and he did not comprehend the sacrifices that Peter and Sabina were making on his behalf. At the beginning of his stay, George behaved badly, and Peter chastised him frequently. On one occasion, a neighbor thought Peter was being overly harsh, even abusive, with the young lad. Peter, on the other hand, felt that George had been brainwashed by the anti-Semitic remarks of the Christians he lived with in Oswiecim. He had spent the last few years as a Catholic, attending Sunday Mass each week with his Catholic guardians. George grew to think of himself as a Catholic and not as a persecuted Jew. Now, after his return to postwar Warsaw, he once again experienced the dangers of being a Jew. One day, realizing the consequences of his Jewish identity, he screamed, "*I don't want to be Jewish!*"

Peter enrolled George in a Jewish parochial school in Warsaw under his real name, George Mandelbaum. It should be no wonder that he was having an identity crisis. On several occasions, he attempted to escape from Peter's care. At other times, he would find an empty lot in which he would camp overnight. On another occasion, he actually tried to join a circus troupe. As one can imagine, he had a strong sense of skepticism: he had suffered the loss of both parents; he had lived in several strange homes; and now, he was expected to adapt to life with two largely unfamiliar adults in a devastated, war-torn city.

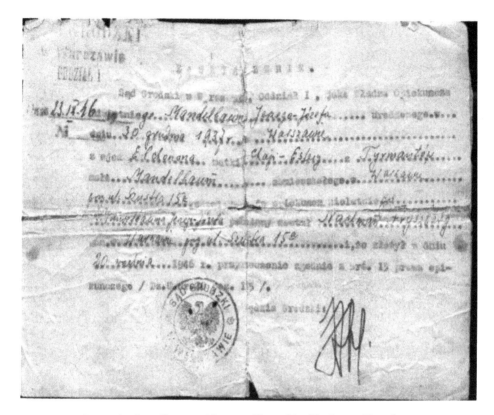

*George's Guardian certificate – Signed by Nachman Fryszberg*

During his eight short years, George experienced many significant changes in his life. These episodes led him to question his identity, and his anger, although misplaced, was nevertheless genuine and understandable. He asked himself many searching questions: Who was his true guardian? Was he Catholic or Jewish? What happened to his father? How long would he remain in this place? What dangers would he face here? All of these uncertainties plagued his mental equilibrium. George had undergone numerous stressful circumstances, and he had experienced many significant losses over his limited years. His level of trust for others was severely compromised due to his varied and unpredictable experiences.

George remained with Peter and Sabina for about eighteen months from early summer 1945 until May 1947. He grew to love Sabina. Although he tested Peter's authority over him at the beginning of his stay, he came to appreciate that his cousin and Sabina had his best interests at heart. During that time, Sabina took care of his physical hygiene making certain he bathed regularly and remained in generally good health. They both worked with George to ensure that he would acquire the necessary verbal and social skills. Peter made sure that George studied and completed his assignments. Nonetheless, they both recognized that the most productive future for George would be in the United States where his cousins Murray and Edna Flug would have the resources to enable George to reach his full potential.

*George while Living with Peter & Sabina in post-war Warsaw*

Sabina was always an attentive listener whenever Peter shared his wartime experiences with her. She promised to stand by him and assist in the completion of his commitment to make certain that young George was settled in a secure place, safe from harm. Peter consistently reminded Sabina of the promise he made to his Uncle Elchanon that Elchanon's only child, would be protected and afforded every possible opportunity to grow as a healthy and successful adult. Sabina also became deeply dedicated to George's welfare. She adopted Peter's commitment to save young George as her commitment also.

Peter and Sabina married in Warsaw in 1949. With Poland in ruins, they decided to immigrate to Israel in 1950. This seemed to Peter to be the most sensible way to escape Warsaw's post-war conditions. Besides, he looked forward to residing in a free and independent Jewish State. At that time, only Jews were authorized to leave Poland to travel to Israel. In order to bring Sabina, a non-Jew, to Israel with him, Peter appealed to a Polish general who knew and liked him. The General gained permission for Sabina to accompany Peter to Israel. Peter knew that Polish citizens who made Israel their permanent residence forfeited their Polish citizenship. But he and Sabina yearned to leave the devastation and oppression of Warsaw even though they would live a Spartan existence in Israel. They could only afford to reside in a tent near the town of Haifa. They resided in a kibbutz which posed difficulties for Sabina since she was unfamiliar with the language, Jewish culture, the climate in Israel, and life in the kibbutz, in general.

Peter secured a basic loan of five hundred dollars through the generosity of the Kacenelenbogen family who were living in Israel. He planned to use the funds to finance a trip to Canada because he believed that, as one of his Canadian friends once expressed, "*You have to scrape your own carrot.*" In other words, one has to fend for oneself. Peter planned to use the money to start a new life, in Canada where Sabina's relatives had settled and felt welcomed. He was indeed planning to pay down the loan as a means of "*scraping his own carrot*".

While in Israel, Peter's family members, the Kacenelenbogens, who had settled in Palestine in the 1930s, were extremely supportive in many ways. In addition to the loan, they provided Sabina with a sewing machine to practice and hone her skills as a dressmaker. They also helped Peter secure training as a heating and air-conditioning technician. He wrote letters to her relatives in Canada and asked about Sabina's sister, Helen, in order to arrange a visit and perhaps to settle near her in Canada. Before she emigrated to Canada in 1945, Helen had been in a German refugee camp. Peter knew that Sabina was anxious to renew her relationship with her sister whom she hadn't seen since they shared their Warsaw apartment. Helen discovered that Sabina and Peter were living in Israel through the information services of the American Red Cross in 1950.

In 1952, Peter and Sabina left Israel and made their way to Naples, Italy. They departed Italy aboard the ship Vulcania and on August 14, 1952 they arrived in Halifax, Nova Scotia. Eventually with the aid of family and the Jewish community, they were drawn to Toronto. Initially, they lived with relatives. Peter and Sabina purchased their first home in Toronto in 1954. They would live there for the next seventeen years. Once they settled in their own home at 280 Wychwood Avenue, Peter used his HVAC skills to secure employment in the field for which he was trained in Israel. Peter worked for the Elder air-conditioning and refrigeration company from 1953-1967. After that he was employed for 17 years (1967-1984) by the Dunham-Bush and Carrier company after Dunham-Bush closed their Canadian operations. Peter managed to learn the business side of heating, ventilation, and air-conditioning (HVAC) over a period of thirty-one years. During his last few years in the job, he was promoted to the role of field supervisor for the Carrier Company.

Peter soon became active in various Jewish organizations and causes. One of those was the Lubliner and UMG Society, a Canadian Jewish organization that dedicated the monument pictured on the next page in memory of his parents among other victims of the Lublin Ghetto. He was

157

dedicated to ensuring that the many sacrifices of his Jewish compatriots were not forgotten. In, Peter attended the dedication of the monument to the Jewish participants in the 1944 Warsaw Uprising. In 2009 Walter's son, George, nominated Peter as a Holocaust survivor who made personal contributions to Ontario, Canada. He also wanted to recognize Peter for saving his father 65 years earlier. The ceremony was officiated by Yad Vashem and the government of Ontario.

*Monument to Victims at Lublin supported by Peter in memory of his Parents*
*Courtesy of the Collection of George Saltzberg*

*Sabina at the Dedication of the Lublin/Trawniki Victims Memorial*
*Courtesy of the Collection of George Saltzberg*

*March of the Ashes Commemorating the Trawniki Victims*
*Courtesy of the Collection of George Saltzberg*

While Peter pursued many worthwhile causes designed to honor victims
and survivors of the Holocaust, Sabina decided to enroll in fashion design
school. She was dedicated to continuing her training as a seamstress, which
she initiated during their time in Israel. Sabina's sister, Helen, made her way
to Canada where they were reunited when Sabina established residence
there. Sabina and Peter obtained a German Shepherd dog named Diana.
Helen's children (Andrew, Basia, and Anna) loved that dog. Sabina sewed
leather booties and a raincoat for the dog. While the girls slept at Sabina's
house, she would often sew them a skirt, a dress or a jumper to surprise
them the following morning. In May, 1955 Sabina served as the Godmother

of Basia, her sister's daughter. She and Peter also attended the Christening of Helen's other daughter, Anna in 1960. Being a Catholic, Sabina treated these services very seriously. She was thrilled to be reunited with Helen and participate in her family's affairs.

Sabina was determined to pay a visit to her parents who were living in Warsaw. Peter tried hard to dissuade her from visiting them because she would have to elude the communists. Nevertheless, he could not deny her desire to connect with her parents. She wanted her mother to know that she was very happy that she married Peter. Her mother had objected vehemently to Sabina's marriage to a Jew. Finally, in the spring of 1966, she convinced Peter to let her make the trip. He conceded to letting her make the arrangements necessary to enter the city of Warsaw, despite his sincere trepidation. He was nervous the entire time she was gone. His fear was that the Communists would detain her and not permit her to return. He knew he would be lost without his Sabina.

Sabina was Christian and Peter, of course, was a Jew. They engaged in many conversations about their religious differences. At times, Peter would offer to convert to Christianity, and Sabina would offer to convert to Judaism. Peter always said, "*Sabina was accepted by my family one hundred percent.*" Sabina decided that she would be the one to convert. This was a complicated decision since her family, especially her mother, was very upset

160

that she married a Jew. In 1980 she secretly took classes when Peter was working out of town. She studied with a local rabbi and without Peter's knowledge she converted to Judaism on July 2, 1980.

When Sabina informed Peter, he was quite angry. He said he really didn't care that she converted. It was Peter's philosophy that there was one God and how you worshipped that deity was unimportant. She was greatly upset by Peter's reaction to her initiative. She burst into tears and told him it was because she loved him. Sabina insisted that since she was accepted so openly in Israel and by Peter's family, she should convert so they could be buried together in a Jewish cemetery and be with each other in the afterlife. She knew that Jewish law would not permit a non-Jew to be buried in a Jewish cemetery.

Peter and Sabina never had children, much to Sabina's disappointment. After having a tubular pregnancy, they made several attempts but Sabina could not bear a child. Peter also confided to George that he was rendered sterile due to medical experimentation on him by the Nazis at one of the camps where he was a captive. Sabina considered adoption but Peter would not condone it. Partially due to their inability to give birth to their own children, Peter and Sabina gifted the Women's and Infant's Maternity Center of the Shaare Zedek Hospital in Canada in the amount of $800,000. Peter had been quite ill when he and Sabina arrived in Israel. He was most grateful for the care he received at the Israel location of the Shaare Zedek Hospital. Their legacy gift was used to create a Well Baby Nursery at the Hospital. George Mandelbaum met with the Hospital's CEO, Dr. Hallevi, to arrange the legacy donation and recognition. He ensured that Peter's will was carried out as indicated.

They also contributed to the Jewish National Fund, Mt. Sinai hospital, Canadian Magen David Adom for Israel. As part of their estate, they provided funding for ambulances to be designed and constructed in Canada and shipped for use to Israel. There, they were retrofitted with the proper cardiac materials and equipment for installation in the ambulances to create a mobile cardiology vehicle. Their plans also provided that the ambulances be replaced in five-year intervals. They also left an endowment to the Gallanough Public Library. That Library enabled Peter to use technology to explore the events of the day, and communicate with other people interested in his life experiences.

Sabina regarded George Mandelbaum as the son she never could have. She made extensive arrangements to welcome him to Canada from New Jersey when he visited each October for Canadian Thanksgiving. She had become very close to George during his time with her and Peter in Warsaw. Sabina was also thrilled to be reunited with her sister Helen and meet her husband Walter immediately following her arrival in Canada. It took a while to re-connect with her other sister, Mila and her husband John Kraszewski in Clinton, Ontario. Finally, in the late 1960s when her other sister Jadwiga Adamowicz immigrated to London, Ontario, they made a point to visit her family, as well. Family was very important to Peter and Sabina since they had both been separated from their relatives. In Peter's case Sabina's siblings were his only family, with the exception of George.

In 1971, Sabina chose a large piece of property for purchase with a small cottage that Peter renovated into a more desirable living space. They planted a vegetable garden and a number of flower beds for her on the property. Their new address was 60 Arnold Avenue in Thornhill, Ontario. They both enjoyed tilling the soil and growing attractive flowers. Sabina worked in that garden throughout the growing season. During the winter she would make preserves that she shared with friends and neighbors. In winter she enjoyed sitting at the picture window and watching the snow fall on the trees outside the addition that Peter built on the house.

*Peter and Sabina's Property & gardens at 60 Arnold Ave. Thornhill, Ontario*

In 2008, Peter was honored at a ceremony sponsored by Yad Vashem and the Government of Ontario. The premier of the Province of Ontario presented Peter with a scroll stipulating "triumph over adversity" representing the theme of Peter's experiences during the war and his activities on behalf of his Jewish brethren

Sabina was diagnosed with Alzheimer's disease in October 2009 at age 88. Peter cared for Sabina at home as the disease gradually invaded her mind. Reluctantly, he decided that she would be better served residing in a nursing home. He committed her to the Valleyview Resident's Center on Finch Avenue in Toronto in January 2011. Peter was diagnosed with bone cancer in February 2011 which compounded his existing condition of prostate cancer. While he waited for a bed to become available, Peter sold their home and moved to the same Valleyview Residence where Sabina was in residence. As soon as Peter arrived at the nursing home to visit her, Sabina questioned him, "Where have you been?". "I have been ill", *he replied.* "I had an operation and stayed in the hospital." She retorted, *"You don't look sick to me."* Lastly, they kissed for what would be the final time they would see each other.

Peter passed away on July 17, 2011 at the age of 90. In March 2011, Walter had flown in from Winnipeg to celebrate the Seder with Peter and other family members. Many tears were shed between Walter and Peter as they recalled the challenges they shared together during the war. This would be their last visit together. Walter knew the end was near for Peter. The previous October, Peter's family and friends arranged a party to celebrate his 90th birthday. Many relatives and friends attended to pay honor and offer respect to Peter. George assembled a special slide show that depicted highlights of Peter's life and times. At the time, they did not realize that he would not celebrate another birthday. His cancer spread throughout his body and in the next year it would end his life.

*Left to Right: Eric Mandelbaum, Peter, George Mandelbaum, Walter Saltzberg and George Saltzberg (standing)*

As he thought back to his many flights from his Nazi oppressors, *Peter expressed the belief that the vast majority of people are well intentioned.* Despite his harrowing encounters, it was his conviction that the majority of people are admirable and represent hope for the human race. He reported, *"These experiences remain with me and continue to disrupt my sleep night after night. I cannot learn how to stop living through it."* However, try as he might, he could not erase the memories of continual pursuit, and the constant stress of taking that one fatal step in the wrong direction. His life and the lives of those he was committed to protect were in peril constantly. The phrase "living on the edge" was definitely applicable to their circumstances.

At the memorial service, Walter Saltzberg's son George delivered the eulogy, reminding people of Peter's bravery during the war. He called to the attention of the assembled congregation the biblical expression, "Whoever saves a life, it is considered as if he saved the entire world." Peter survived two ghetto residences (Lublin and Warsaw) and two concentration camps (DAW at Majdanek and Trawniki). As Walter once said, "Peter was the most resourceful man I have ever met."

Sabina passed away three years after Peter in January 2014. She and her husband had enjoyed 63 years of marriage. According to her wishes, she had a typical Jewish funeral service and was buried with her beloved

Nachman side by side in the Toronto Jewish burial grounds.

*Peter and Sabina at his seventy-eighth birthday, October 9, 1998*
*Picture Courtesy of George Mandelbaum*

# Chapter Fourteen

## George's Life in London, 1947–1951

*"We are what is left of a people that were not able to celebrate the Jewish religion because another government decided that we were not worth existing, much less openly practicing our faith."*

*—Hanna Keselman, Holocaust survivor as a "hidden child"*

On May 9, 1947, Peter arranged for George to travel from Warsaw to Danzig and then to London, England, with a stopover in Edinburgh, Scotland through the Hebrew Immigrant Aid Society (HIAS). The arrangements had to be made in secret because the Communists prohibited Polish citizens from leaving the country. Now that the war was over, Peter wanted George to study at a Yeshiva in England. He was able to enroll George, who was nearly ten years old, in the Ahavas Torah Boarding School on 93 Stamford Hill in London.

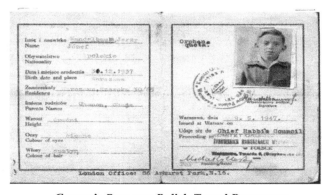

***George's Post-war Polish Travel Document***

George departed for England from the port of Gdansk on the Baltic Sea. Before leaving, Peter asked his cousin to write to him on a regular basis. But writing letters was not part of George's regular habits. Very few letters were sent to Peter from George. He did not mean to be disrespectful; he simply had not learned the discipline of letter writing. Moreover, George was far from a model student. He had refused to do homework even while he was living with Peter and Sabina and attending school in Warsaw. He was not diligent about his studies. Peter purchased a dog in the hope that the dog would cajole George into studying out of gratitude. George named the dog Mika. However, the dog had no effect on George's study habits.

At Ahavas Torah, George also presented various disciplinary challenges to his teachers. He did manage to learn basic skills and to comprehend and speak British English at a basic literacy level during his four-year stay. He was taught English, mathematics, and Hebrew in multi-age classes. However, academically, he did the absolute minimum. Being rather big for his age, he possessed a physical advantage over his peers and little tolerance for teasing. So, he willingly engaged in fist fighting at the slightest provocation. George enjoyed the British, but he did not adopt their proclivity for academic pursuits.

George made an acquaintance with another young man named Alex Rajinski who was also from Poland. He and George kept up their friendship

170

over many years. Even when Alex changed his surname from Rajinski to Raden. Like George, Alex lost his father in the Holocaust. They met each other in Poland waiting for transportation to England. When George flew from Warsaw to Gdansk, he reconnected with Alex for the shipboard journey from Gdansk to Edinburgh, and they traveled together on the train to London. George appreciated Alex's companionship during their lengthy trip. They lost contact with each other after arriving in London. However, many years later, George discovered that his friend had become a chaplain at Brandeis University.

The students at Ahavas Torah Boarding School came from many different countries, including Poland. There were also some young people from the British Isles. Though it was a religious school where the common bond was Judaism, the school followed the British national curriculum. George's dormitory room housed four or more students, depending on the total enrollment at the time. The rooms had fireplaces, which the students had to ignite and maintain. There was a dining room on the ground floor of the dormitory building where meals were served. The staff was firm but fair and caring. George often fell into disfavor with the school's faculty and administration. He did not act in keeping with the expectations for the typical student. Academic difficulties soon arose due to his frequent behavioral outbursts.

George realized that he was probably the only true orphan among his schoolmates. Most of the others had only lost one parent or were among the so-called "hidden children". (Children whose parent(s) arranged for them to be placed in the care of another family, often a non-Jewish household, to ensure their safety for the duration of the war.) Their plan was to retrieve their children when the Nazi threat had dissipated. Unfortunately, many of these parents did not survive the war and the Holocaust. Thus, many of the children were, in fact, orphans at the end of the war. George was both an orphan and a "hidden child" when he lived in Osweicom.

The school in London had strict curfews for bedtime and playtime. Even though the blitzkrieg had ended, caution and school rules remained in effect. George received packages of treats and clothes frequently from Murray Flug and his family in Brooklyn, New York. Much to his chagrin, Peter did not receive many letters from George, who was not inclined to write and too busy playing. Oftentimes, play consisted of manipulating cardboard boxes the children discovered in the school's backyard. The children built play houses from the boxes; and played war games with them manipulating the boxes as if they were tanks.

George gradually became somewhat conversant with the King's English. He even acquired a distinct British accent. When the opportunity arose, he was occasionally invited to spend the weekend with a British family willing to take him in as a guest. On a weekly basis, he would visit the public baths in London to bathe and swim. He enjoyed these opportunities immensely. He soon discovered a local bicycle shop where the owner invited him to help repair bikes. In return for his labor, he was granted the opportunity to ride a bicycle through London. He rode around town as a means of familiarizing himself with this world class albeit shell-shocked city. In fact, he enjoyed a good degree of independence in London.

# Chapter Fifteen

## George's Life in the United States

*"No matter where you live, where you come from, what language you speak, what religion that you subscribe to . . . we're all the same people."*

—*Ray Allen, professional basketball player*

George would have been eligible to become a British citizen in 1952. However, in late 1950, Peter informed George that the Flugs had arranged for his transportation to the United States on the ocean liner, the *Queen Mary*, departing from Southampton, England on January 31, 1951. He was beside himself feeling very mixed emotions. Once again, in his short life, he was being plucked from familiar surroundings to travel to another unknown and unfamiliar place of residence.

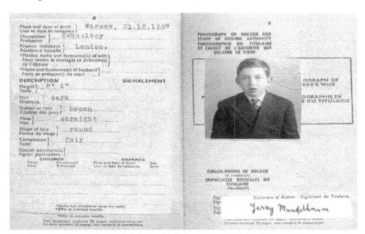

***George's British Travel Documents***

He had found the British to be most hospitable and he was resentful of being requested to depart for another change in his surroundings. In London, he was able to take day trips to the countryside on weekends. George had a real sense of independence and comfort due to his ability to travel alone, unfettered by strict rules. He realized, however, that the Flugs were family members who would most likely welcome him and he looked forward to seeing the United States, the country he had heard so much about. Therefore, he consented to the move.

George's stateroom was located on the lowest deck of the vessel. Yet, he made it his quest to become acquainted with someone who had much more luxurious accommodations and was willing to share the advantages. Many of the steerage passengers schmoozed with those of a more privileged status during their voyage in order to gain more desirable advantages. George happened to be successful in his effort at gaining the favor of one particular woman. The woman was obviously much more affluent and could afford to treat George to some of the finer trappings the ocean liner had to offer. He flattered her with his lavish expression of appreciation for each token of generosity. She invited him to join her for several sumptuous meals. One day, the woman asked George if he would do her a favor. She requested that he wear a watch she carried with her and keep it on his person until he reached his destination in Brooklyn. She would then visit him at his aunt and uncle's home and retrieve the watch. He shared the Brighton Beach address of his aunt, Rachel Mandelbaum Flug, with the woman as she requested. Within a few weeks after he arrived at that address, the woman telephoned his aunt and scheduled a time to visit to reclaim the watch. George never knew the significance of the piece of jewelry or, whether it contained anything of import. He just kept his word and turned it over to the woman when she arrived, as he had promised.

George was able to immigrate to the United States due to the collaborative efforts of his cousins: Nachman Fryzsberg, aka Peter Jablonski, Jan and Marila Szarkowski, and Murray Flug. Murray emigrated to New York before his parents at age 24. He was George's first cousin and the son of his Aunt Rachel and her husband, Abraham. Elchanon had arranged the Flugs' safe passage to the United States before the outbreak of the war. They lived in Brooklyn, New York. Rachel had been an important ally in Elchanon's precious metals business. Elchanon had also assisted in arranging safe passage to Mexico for his cousins Esther and Sarah. After five years of residence and successful completion of a citizenship test, Murray and Rachel were issued their certifications for citizenship.

No. 5729999

Name ..... FLUG Rachel ..............................................

residing at .. 110 Division Ave Bk ...........................

Age 57 ...... years. Date of order of admission Dec 27th 1943 ...

Date certificate issued Dec 27th 1943 .......................... by the

U. S. District ............ Court at ...... Brooklyn, New York ........

Petition No. 393147

AR#3583166          x   *Rachel - Flug*
                        (Complete and true signature of holder)

No. 4308213

Name ..... FLUG Murray ............................................

residing at 110 Division Ave. Bk. ..........................

Age 29 ....... years. Date of order of admission Mar. 14, 1939

Date certificate issued ...... Mar. 14, 1939 .......... by the

U. S. District ........ Court at ........ Brooklyn, New York ......

Petition No. 288716

                    *Murray Flug*
                    (Complete and true signature of holder)

*Certification of Citizenship for Rachel Flug and Her Son Murray Flug.*
*Courtesy of US Immigration Service and Ancestry. Com*

George arrived in New York harbor on a cold and foggy day. He had

wanted to take a picture of the much renowned Statue of Liberty as he

entered the harbor, but it was obscured by the fog. He disembarked from the

*Queen Mary* at Pier 93 on February 5, 1951. He was classified as a

Displaced Person (DP). His cousin, Murray Flug, Rachel, and Murray's son

Howard met him at the pier. There his aunt Rachel Mandelbaum Flug

greeted him enthusiastically. She hugged him so tightly he almost choked.

177

Murray drove George and the family along the West Side Highway through the Brooklyn Battery Tunnel into the borough of Brooklyn. He also met Murray's wife, Edna, and their three other sons, Leonard, Eric, and Marshal. Many other members of the family and friends came to celebrate George's arrival. Following his welcome, Murray took George to clothiers on the lower east side of Manhattan to outfit him with new clothes from head to toe.

*Passenger manifest with Jerzyk, aka George, Mandelbaum, of the Queen Mary's voyage from Southampton, England, to New York, January 31–February 5, 1951.*

Murray and Edna Flug lovingly took George into their home and raised him as if he was their own son. Their four sons accepted him as another brother. The embrace of George by his adopted siblings was a great source of comfort and companionship for an orphaned boy. It became a relationship he has retained throughout his life. To this day, George remains fast friends with his four Flug "brothers", as he refers to them. Each of the four also enjoyed great success in their careers. Leonard became a respected dentist; Howard was an engineer; Eric became a successful Pediatrician; and, Marshal also entered the field of engineering. Together they regularly visit Murray and Edna Flug's gravesite in New Jersey to pay tribute to the "brothers" biological and surrogate parents' lives.

Murray and Edna's family realized the hardships George had endured, especially his loss of both parents. They were ready and able to shelter George and prepare him for a productive future. Peter had made them aware of his talents and as they recognized his potential, the Flugs were committed to providing a proper education for him to further develop his ability. Murray's wife, Edna, tutored him in American English for six months to prepare him for admission to Abraham Lincoln High School in Brooklyn in September 1951. He had only completed the equivalent of sixth grade while in England and, yet, he was expected to pass an entrance exam for Lincoln High School in the spring without benefit of a seventh and eighth grade experience.

Murray and Edna soon learned that George would not be an easy young man to convince of the value of education. He was more interested in girls than he was committed to his studies. Murray was often summoned to the principal's office during George's early high school years. George was inclined to get into fights, or he violated one or another of the school's rules. On many occasions, other students mimicked George's manner of speech because of his British accent. George was rather big for his age and he did not tolerate bullying well. At Rachel Flug's insistence, George also attended the Lubavitcher Yeshiva in Brooklyn.

No. 7599817

Name..MANDELBAUM George Joseph

residing at..215 Westend Avenue...Brooklyn

Date of birth...12-31-37.. Date of order of admission...5-22-56

Date certificate issued.........May 22, 1956.............by the

........U. S. District....Court at......Brooklyn, New York

Petition No......

Alien Registration No. A7 959 928

*(Complete and true signature of holder)*

**George Mandelbaum's Certification for Citizenship**

On May 22, 1956, George became a US citizen. After graduating simultaneously from Abraham Lincoln High School and Lubavitch Yeshiva in June 1955, he started his college career at City College of New York in September 1955 before transferring to Pratt Institute in Brooklyn in 1957.

He matriculated in the evening division of Pratt from 1957-1965. While he was still pursuing his degree at Pratt, he decided to join the United States Air Force (USAF) and avoided the draft and possible assignment to another branch of the armed forces. He wished to give back to the country he loved and felt compelled to serve. Because he harbored an interest in flying and he was committed to serving his adopted nation, he chose to serve six years in the Air Force (1959-1965). He served on Active and Reserve duty during military service in the Air Force. He became qualified as a pilot while in the service of his adopted country. Eventually, George returned to Pratt to complete his degree in design and construction after earning his honorable discharge from the USAF. By then, he had become a much more serious student and he comported himself very well, academically.

While he was taking evening courses at Pratt and before he joined the USAF, George secured an intern position with the architectural firm of Max Simon architects. There he encountered an employee of the firm by the name of Gerald Vickers. Vickers was a taskmaster who insisted on perfection in every detail of design and drawings. If George made a mistake that threatened to inhibit productivity, Mr. Vickers would require him to remain after hours to adjust the error on his own time. George considered Vickers to be his most valued mentor and the person who taught him the kind of resiliency necessary for his success in the architectural field. He continued to learn on the job while attending evening classes by working with Charles Luckman Associates in New York City. The highlights of his association with Luckman was the opportunity to work on the 1964-65 World's Fair in Flushing Meadows and Madison Square Garden in Manhattan. George was awarded a Robert Moses Recognition Award for his contribution to the 1964 World's Fair project. He was thrilled to be able to contribute to that endeavor.

Peter advised George regarding the location of property that his father had purchased in Israel before the war. Indeed, he located the property in Natania a suburb of Tel Aviv. George sold the property in Israel, in 1972. He recalls this date of sale vividly because while he was traveling from Israel to Munich he realized the Olympic games were in progress. He arrived in Munich on September 6, the day of the so-called Munich Massacre as eleven Israeli athletes were murdered by a Palestinian terrorist group. That event reminded him that the threat to Jewish people was still real. George heard of the massacre on his way to attend the Olympic Games and ordered his cab driver to return to the airport, where he boarded a plane to fly back home to the United States. During 1973-1977, he was a partner with Sage Design Corporation in Rockland County, New York.

George worked on several projects in Israel. In one instance he was hired as Project Manager for a phase of construction of an air field under the auspices of Negev Airbase Constructors. It was due to his international experience in Israel that he secured a position with Metca USA. For thirteen years (1979-1992), George worked for Metca, USA in a few months the position was transferred to the London-based subsidiary known as Metca UK Ltd. He served as the Company Director and Chief Operating Officer. He completed his design and construction career with Tri-Net/Meadowview Construction in Somerset, NJ and he retired from Bayport Construction Company in Brooklyn, NY in 2018. George's career and personal interests took him all over the world. He had assignments and interests in Israel, Saudi Arabia, Kuwait, Turkey, and other Mideast and European countries. The orphaned young boy persisted and became a highly successful professional man who was capable of accomplishments in the United States and worldwide.

In the summer of 1956 as soon as George could afford a car, he drove his DeSoto to Canada to visit Peter and Sabina. At other times, he piloted his own airplane to make the trip. George made annual trips to Canada to visit with his cousin and to find out the details of how Peter arranged George's escape from Warsaw and the many significant events in their lives. Much of their conversations centered around the events of the war especially those that George was too young to remember, or missed while he was in hiding. Peter also told George about his father of whom

George had little direct knowledge. Most of these particulars were unknown to George due to his age at the time and his lack of involvement or knowledge of the planning that was involved. He was too young to recall many of the details and unable to realize their significance at the time they occurred. Peter filled in the gaps that existed in George's memory. They engaged in long walks around his Canadian neighborhood. He introduced George to his neighbors and friends and the places where he spent his days. Peter always had a project in the works. He made sculpture figures from scraps of copper materials that he gathered from the scrap heap at work. They talked of books and the current news. At times he would demonstrate his guitar and banjo playing to George. As Peter's illnesses advanced, George's visits by auto or airplane became more frequent. They became not simply cousins but fast friends.

George traveled to Warsaw several times in an effort to reclaim his family's property rights to the building at Smulikowskiego 7. For over 50 years he has been pursuing a legal action against the Polish government in an effort to redeem the value of that property. On one of those occasions, he met Yale Reisner of the Ronald S. Lauder Foundation Genealogy Project at the Jewish Historical Institute Archives in Warsaw. Reisner, the director of research and archives, was able to provide George with several documents found in their collection relating to George's experiences in Poland. (See

Appendix A.) These documents verified George's status as an orphan and included his medical reports as well as an intelligence test administered to him in 1946. The documents also proved that George survived the war under the Aryan name Jan Szarkowski. It is noteworthy that George was originally scheduled to migrate to Mexico in 1947. Peter was able to revise that destination so that George traveled to the United States from England as a displaced person to live with the Flugs.

After gaining much experience, George's architectural partnership was restructured into a design and construction practice. George retired from the construction business in the United States in 2018. He continues to do consulting design and construction work in New York and volunteer work in New Jersey. He lives with his wife, Bonnie, a successful real estate agent, in New Jersey. He has two married children, Eric, a professor of dental surgery at Boston University and Allison, a former vice-president for hospital administration at Parkway Hospital in Queens, N.Y. Allison resigned her position to raise her children. They have blessed George with four grandchildren, Joshua who lives in Boston, Benjamin serving in the military, Zachary who resides in New York City, and Rayna who is matriculating in a Masters' program at Lehigh University. Their ages range from 22-25. Each one is a successful professional with a college degree.

George recalls his two children being born at the Brooklyn Jewish hospital and delivered by a Dr. Nachamie. His first born, Eric, was brought into the world on a cold December 28, 1963. He remembers driving home to his apartment at 820 Ocean Parkway through Prospect Park on a roadway freshly covered with about three inches of snow. His tire tracks were the first impressions in the snow. It was a beautiful feeling, he recalled. When he went to sleep he remembers having a nightmare wherein a young child was standing over his grave asking, "Daddy why did you leave?" He woke up and never got back to sleep, returning to the hospital to be with the child and his mother. He attributed this dream to reflections of the loss of his mother at an early age. In January 1965 when his daughter Allison was born, recovery was in the same room as Eric's and the celebratory champagne cork from Eric was found in the room's chandelier. This time there was no nightmare of Allison standing over his grave. George was very much devoted to his little girl and would become very protective of her.

# Chapter Sixteen

## The Postwar Years: Walter and Michelina

Early in 1945, Peter contacted the World Jewish Congress to seek help for Walter Saltzberg. They referred him to the Central Committee of Jews in Poland who ran several homes for children who were displaced during the war. With their help, when the war officially ended in Europe, he brought Walter to the Jewish orphanage in Otwock, fourteen miles southeast of Warsaw, which was established to care for the child survivors. It was not an easy feat given Walter's badly injured leg that had gone for two years without medical treatment. Doctors in a Russian military hospital in Otwock operated on Walter's leg with poor results. Many months later, doctors in Sweden refractured and reset the distorted leg, which yielded some success. Little is certain regarding his travels to Stockholm for the surgery, except that he was accompanied by a friend from Jerusalem, Ruth Berlinger who visited him in the hospital in Sweden. However, his leg never knitted together uniformly. It would remain distorted and shorter than the other one, giving Walter a permanent limp and the need to wear a specially constructed shoe to gain some equilibrium.

While Walter was residing in the Jewish orphanage in Otwock, several American reporters came to interview young people about their wartime experiences. Fortunately, they chose Walter as one of the interviewees and published his interview. A former friend of his parents, Meyer Schwartzapel, recognized his name when he happened to read the story in a Yiddish newspaper shared with him by a friend. Schwartzapel had assumed that none of the Saltzberg family members had survived. He hurriedly arranged for Walter to immigrate to Winnipeg, Canada in order to join his distant relatives there. Walter arrived at Pier 21 in Halifax, Nova Scotia, on December 2, 1947, about a month shy of his seventeenth birthday. Several relatives who had been advised of his arrival by Mr. Schwartzapel, met him at the pier to welcome him and assist him with settlement in his new country.

At this point in his life, Walter had no more than a second-grade education. He settled in Winnipeg, Manitoba, Canada, where he lived with the Chmelnitsky family and attended school. Mrs. Chmelnitsky was a widow who ran a Jewish catering business and a boarding house. She began taking in young Jewish boys when the Winnipeg Orphanage closed, and the need of homes for Jewish youth such as Walter remained. Walter found the care and shelter of the boarding house preferable to the orphanage at Otwock. He was welcomed by his hostess and fed most generously. Walter gradually regained his strength and became used to the strained mobility

caused by his surgically-repaired leg and the adjustment required by his

augmented shoe.

Just ten years later, in 1957, he earned a bachelor's degree in civil

engineering from the University of Manitoba. Soon after graduation, he

began a forty-plus years' career with the Manitoba Department of Highways

and Transportation and eventually became the director of bridges and

structures for the Province of Manitoba. After he retired in 1997, Walter

became an international liaison officer with the ISIS Research Network and

an associate professor and engineer-in-residence at the University of

Manitoba. Walter married and had three children, George, Jack, and Anna,

with his first wife, Joan Carole Gordon. One of his children developed

schizophrenia. Because of her affliction Walter devoted much of his spare

time advocating for better acceptance and understanding of this mental

illness. He became president of the Manitoba Schizophrenia Society and

second vice president of the Schizophrenia Society of Canada. He

participated in many other humanitarian efforts and Holocaust

remembrances.

Walter spoke publicly at schools and civic events about his experiences

during the war, hoping it would inspire tolerance in people of various

religious beliefs. He also wished to acknowledge those individuals who, at the peril of their own lives, saved his life and the lives of others. First, Dr. Kazimierz Wiechowski, the Christian doctor who smuggled him out of the Warsaw Ghetto when Walter was eleven years old and kept him hidden in his home for two years. It was at the peril of his own life that the good doctor protected Walter from the Nazis. Yad Vashem honored Walter's protector at a ceremony in Israel, as a "Righteous among Nations" award recipient. This recognition was granted to non-Jews who took exceptional risks to protect Jewish refugees. Peter Jablonski, aka Nachman Fryzsberg, was his other hero. He had dug Walter from the rubble and cared for him in the makeshift shelter that he built. Peter obtained medical treatment for Walter's severely injured leg and, he found a home for Walter after their liberation. Peter made certain that Walter was secure in an orphanage before he left to take care of his own injuries.

Walter died on March 8, 2018; both his first wife, Joan Carole Gordon, and his second wife, Sheila Greenberg Smith, predeceased him. He recounted that his constant and haunting fantasy during his plight was simply his longing for one glass of clear, cold drinking water.

**Michelina**

Michelina Poacyliusz was an unusual, caring person who did whatever she could for oppressed people. During the war, she had risked her life without any financial remuneration but with great personal commitment.

Peter never forgot her generosity, and he was extremely grateful for her unwavering support of him and his fellow refugees in hiding. He recalled that the AK stopped her on one occasion and called her "a Jewish *kurwa* (whore)" as they shot at her. They missed Michelina but killed her dog. This event was a source of great anguish to Michelina for she was devoted to her Lordzio and to rescuing all peoples, regardless of their background. She took the dog's body into the woods to provide a respectful burial for it. Eventually, she had to flee from her persistent tormentors by hiding herself away at a cabin in the countryside where, with her husband Anton at her side, she died of cancer. Many years later, when Sabina was visiting her parents in Poland, she stopped first at Anton Poacyliusz's home with gifts for him. She stayed there for two days while he regaled her with stories of Michelina's final days. She listened intently to his respectful recollections of his wife before she traveled on to visit her own parents. Michelina was a true protector of those who were threatened and demeaned by the Nazis and their oppressive ideology.

# Afterword

It is gratifying to know that the three principals in this document have enjoyed success in their careers in the wake of the experiences they survived during the war years when the Holocaust was raging all around them. Walter became a successful engineer and public administrator. Peter was an effective, long-serving field supervisor with the Carrier Company, and George launched a productive architectural and construction career with an international reach. George and Walter persisted in their loyalty to Peter remaining indebted to him for his courageous protection and support during all the years since their shared torment by the Nazis. Peter was grateful for the warm hospitality of the Mandelbaum family toward Regina and him when they arrived in Warsaw. Walter expressed his gratitude for Peter's persistent care and deliverance to proper medical treatment. Peter would not leave Walter's side until he found a place for him to live. George came to realize the safety and security that Peter and Sabina provided to him, and how they made certain he was delivered to a suitable pathway for his future accomplishments.

The counterbalance to these tales of protection and security is the fate of the many who could have realized similar potentials had they been as fortunate to survive as these three. How many more Albert Einsteins, Elie

Weisels, or Viktor Frankls might have emerged from among the hundreds of thousands of Jews whose lives were taken from them, and the rest of us by the Nazi killing machine? The potential of those who were slaughtered in the name of a misguided political philosophy is staggering. Those Jews and other victims who were protected by others, like Peter Jablonski, can be eternally grateful for the lives they were able to reclaim through the heroism of people who were tenacious and incorruptible.

Peter was not only resourceful he was possessed of a moral fiber that suffused his entire being. He acted in the manner that Ted Kennedy expressed in his eulogy of his brother, Robert, "Some men see things as they are and ask 'Why?' Others dream dreams that never were and ask, 'Why not?'." Peter was a person who saw the needs of his fellow man or woman and responded with deep conviction. He never asked *why*, he was too preoccupied with finding out *how*.

Now that Peter and Walter are deceased, only George remains. It was his vow to Peter, to use the autobiographical record that Peter prepared, to write a book worthy of their experiences. This writer was genuinely humbled to be asked by George Mandelbaum to write this inspiring story of the intersecting lives of three Holocaust survivors. As the primary author and a Christian, I have been privileged to come to learn much more about the

Holocaust and the unique sacrifices made by so many who came to know

the face of evil while they survived and protected one another.

John R. McIntyre

# ADDITIONAL PHOTOS

*Memorial to Trawniki Ghetto Victims*
*Courtesy of George Mandelbaum 2001*

*Memorial to Victims of the Warsaw Uprising*
*Courtesy of George Mandelbaum 2001*

*Memorial to Victims of the Warsaw Ghetto Courtesy of George Mandelbaum 2001*

*George at Warsaw Synagogue of his Childhood - 2001*

*Peter at Hero's Monument Dedication*
*Perrsonal collection of George Saltzberg*

*Peter's Canadian Identification Card*
*Courtesy of George Saltzberg*

*Peter Jablonski – Before, During, & After the War with His Mother*
*Courtesy of George Saltzberg*

# Appendix A

## The Ronald S. Lauder Foundation Genealogy Project
## at the Jewish Historical Institute of Poland
ul. Tłomackie 3/5, 00-090 Warsaw, POLAND
tel.: (48-22) 827-9221; fax: (48-22) 827-1843; e-mail: laudergen@jewish.org.pl

Warsaw, 1 August 2001
12 Menachem Av 5761

Mr. George Mandelbaum
43 Louis Drive
Montville, NJ 07045 USA

Dear Mr. Mandelbaum:

It was a pleasure meeting you in Warsaw. I hope your visit here proved interesting and trust your journey home was safe and pleasant.

Further to our conversation, I am forwarding several documents found in the Jewish Historical Institute Archives which appear to concern you personally.

They are as follows:

1) Your registration with the Warsaw Jewish Committee on Targowa Street in the Praga District on 27 April 1946. It shows your birthdate as 30 December 1937 and indicates that you survived the war on so-called "Aryan" papers as Jan Szarkowski. It also provides your parents' names and your pre- and post-war addresses;
2) An enlargement of your photo from the Jewish Health Care Association [Towarzystwo Ochrony Zdrowia] archives;
3) The complete document bearing the above-mentioned photograph. It lists you as a "complete orphan," i.e. neither parent survived;
4) Your request to the Jewish Child Care Department for winter clothing (28 November 1946);
5) Your medical reports from 1946;
6) An intelligence test administered to you in fourth grade.
7) A letter to Mr. Nachman Fryszberg-Jabłoński, indicating that you were being prepared for migration to Mexico (21 January 1947).

I hope you find these documents of interest.

Sincerely,

Yale J. Reisner, Director of Research & Archives, Ronald S. Lauder Foundation

# Appendix B

## The Holocaust: Facts and Figures

While approximately 299,500 Jews from the Warsaw Ghetto and its environs died in the Treblinka gas chambers in the 60-day period from July 22 to September 21, 1942, some never made it alive to the camps. In their already weakened condition, they could not tolerate the extreme heat or the illnesses that were extant in the close environment of the freight trains. The smells from perspiration and human excrement were intolerable. Jews were also misled, being told that they were being "resettled," a euphemism for death by lethal gas, or by the cruel and often fatal treatment by the Nazis in the camps. On one occasion, July 29, 1943, knowing that starvation was rampant, the Germans posted the promise of 3 kilograms of bread and 1 kilogram of marmalade to volunteers for "resettlement." Using this tactic, the Germans distributed 180,000 kilograms of bread and 36,000 kilograms of marmalade, yielding the calculable number of deaths.

The daily food rationing for Jews living in the ghetto averaged 181 calories. The Nazis had created a diabolical means of achieving gradual murder through starvation. The monthly mortality rate rose from 898 in January 1941 to a high of 5,560 by January 1942. The average mortality rate during that period was 3,882 victims per month. Illness and various forms of maltreatment abounded. These circumstances seriously affected the physical and mental welfare of the Jewish inhabitants of the ghetto.

Altogether, the Germans delivered some 43,500 Jews by train from the Lublin district to the death camp at Belzec from March through December 1942; contrary to the Nazi's assurances that they were being sent to a labor camp. In May 1942, the Nazis opened another death camp called Sobibor where a great many Lublin Jews transmigrated. At least 100,000 Jews from Lublin were exterminated at the Sobibor death camp during the period May 1942 through January 1943. Sobibor divided inmates into three levels of punitive facilities. Camp I was where all Jews slept and some worked. Camp II was where they stored materials (clothes, money, and jewelry) stolen from the Jews and some additional jobs were carried out, and Camp III housed six gas chambers and other killing methods.

*Jewish Cemetery adjacent to Warsaw Ghetto – Courtesy of George Mandelbaum 2001*

*Bunker of ZOB Leader Mordechaj Anielewicz marking the*
*Headquarters for the Jewish Uprising known as Mila 18*
*Anielewicz committed suicide on May 8, 1943.*
*Courtesy of George Mandelbaum 2001*

*Memorial to the Path of the 300,000 Jews shipped by rail to the Death Camps from the*
*Umschlagplatz in the Warsaw Ghetto*

203

# Source Materials

Campbell, J. (1990). The Hero's Journey. New York: Harper Collins.

Holocaust Education and Archive Research Team, "The Warsaw Ghetto."
http://www.holocaustresearchproject.org/ghettos/warsawghetto.html

Jablonski, P. Notes on Experience in World War II. February 18, 2000.

Jagielski, Jan, and Robert Pasieczny, *A Guide to Jewish Warsaw*. Warsaw,
Poland: Jewish Information and Tourist Bureau, 1990.

Lichtenstein, Ruth (editor),( 2009). *Witness to History*. Brooklyn, NY:
Project Witness.

Marks, Jane, (1993). *Hidden Children: The Secret Survivors of the
Holocaust*. New York: Fawcett.

Minuk, S. (n.d.) *Legacy gift from holocaust survivor and his wife*. Shaare
Zedek Hospital Foundation

Rashke, Richard, (1982). *Escape from Sobibor*. Boston, MA: Houghton
Mifflin Co.

Sakowska, Ruth, (2001). *The Warsaw Ghetto: 1940–1945*. Warsaw, Poland:
Drakpol.

Saltzberg, G. Personal communication with George Mandelbaum, October
12, 2019

Schiller, R. (August 11, 2011). Newpaper article transforms lives of holocaust
survivors, not once but twice. Forward, YIVO Institute for Jewish
Research

Statement from the Press Secretary. August 21, 2018. The White House:
Office of the Press Secretary

"Tobbens and Schultz: Nazi German textile manufacturer."
https://peoplepill.com/people/toebbens-and-schultz/

Wojtas, B. Sabina's Story personal communication, September 16, 2019

# ABOUT THE AUTHOR

John R. McIntyre is Professor Emeritus at Caldwell University. At the University level he has taught undergraduate and graduate courses for the past 25 years. He currently advises doctoral candidates who are writing their dissertations. John has enjoyed a career in education that spanned over 55 years. His roles have included classroom teacher through superintendent of schools. Dr. McIntyre taught at Saint Peter's University prior to Caldwell University. His previous writings have been exclusively in the form of articles and book chapters for professional journals and books. This is his first full length non-fiction book. John lives with his wife Patricia in Montville, New Jersey. They have been married for 57 years and have three sons: John, Kevin, and Glenn and nine grandchildren. John is proud that George Mandelbaum, his friend and neighbor, entrusted him to help fulfill his promise to publish and distribute Peter Jablonski's story. As Peter suggested, unless it is written down, no one will believe it happened.

Made in the USA
Las Vegas, NV
18 July 2021